Tragedy and Hope 101

The Illusion of Justice, Freedom, and Democracy

Joseph Plummer

Introduction by G. Edward Griffin

Acknowledgements

First, I want to sincerely thank *you* for investing your time and money into researching (and resisting) corporate and state-sponsored crime. Without people like you, the world would be a very ugly place.

Second, I'd like to thank all of the authors who've contributed to this field of knowledge. From Quigley, Kissinger, Bernays and Russell, to Griffin, Ganser, Allen and Engdahl; this book would not have been possible without your work.

Last but not least, I'd like to thank GoBerkey.com and Darol Johnson for their financial contribution to this project.

Contents

Introduction

by G. Edward Griffin

If you have ever watched an illusionist perform up-close magic, you know the power of misdirection and sleight of hand. Even in a room full of suspicious and attentive observers, the illusionist can fool them all. By exploiting known weaknesses in the human mind and employing his tools of the trade, he will deceive the crowd whether it wants to be deceived or not.

Imagine what an equally talented "network" of political illusionists can accomplish. Performing before an audience of mostly trusting and casual observers, exploiting known weaknesses in the human mind, and employing their tools of the trade, they, too, will deceive the crowd whether it wants to be deceived or not.

Having spent nearly sixty years of my life researching and writing about the illusionists who control our world, I can say without reservation that you are about to learn some of their closest-held secrets. Joe has done an outstanding job of weeding through Carroll Quigley's book, *Tragedy & Hope*. He has captured the essence of what Quigley referred to as "the Network" and made this important information accessible to the average person who simply doesn't have time to read a 1,300-page history book. Even for those who intend to read the entire volume, Joe has created an introduction and study guide that will serve the serious student well.

Knowledge of who Carroll Quigley was and the deceptions that he revealed is essential for understanding the real world of today. His close relationship with the Network and his approval of its aims made it possible to provide an insider's analysis of the minds and methods of the global elite. Without this knowledge, the actions of those who dominate the US government and the Western world do not make sense. With it, everything falls into place.

Be forewarned. The journey you are about to begin is not for the fainthearted. If you are comfortable with the illusions that currently pass for political reality, this book is not for you, because, once you discover how the deceivers perform their magic, the comfort of ignorance is no longer possible. Once the bell is rung, it cannot be unrung.

The bell starts ringing on the next page.

G. Edward Griffin
October 4, 2013

CHAPTER 1
Democracy

Have you ever felt like democracy is just an illusion? Have you ever suspected that there are very "powerful people" who've created a system that *appears* to be democratic, but actually cuts ordinary citizens out of the decision-making process? Have you ever wondered: "Who is really running things, and what exactly are they trying to achieve?" If you have, you're not alone.

Fortunately, a Harvard-educated history professor named Carroll Quigley wrote a handful of books that answer all of these questions and more. Unfortunately, the answers are very disturbing, especially to those who've accepted the common myths of "democratic government."

In Quigley's work we discover that national constitutions are routinely undermined by the leaders who are elected to defend them. We learn that "all social instruments tend to become institutions," regardless of their benevolent origin, and, from that point forward, the *institution* is run for the benefit of those who control it (at the expense of its original purpose).[1]

Perhaps most unsettling, Quigley reveals that real power operates behind the scenes, in secrecy, and with little to fear from so-called democratic elections. He proves that conspiracies, secret societies, and small, powerful networks of

---

1 Quigley, *Evolution of Civilizations*, page 101

individuals are not only real; they're extremely effective at creating or destroying entire nations and shaping the world as a whole. We learn that "representative government" is, at best, a carefully managed con game.

Since these disturbing truths contradict nearly everything our government, education system, and media have taught us to believe, many will immediately dismiss them as nonsense. "Only wild-eyed conspiracy theorists believe such things," they will say. However, there is one big problem: Carroll Quigley was no wild-eyed conspiracy theorist. Quite the contrary, Quigley was a prominent historian who specialized in studying the evolution of civilizations as well as secret societies. He studied history at Harvard University, where he earned his bachelor's, master's, and PhD degrees. He taught at Princeton University, Harvard University, and the School of Foreign Service at Georgetown University. He worked as an advisor to the US Defense Department, the US Navy, and the Smithsonian Institution.[2]

In short, Carroll Quigley was a well-connected and well-credentialed member of Ivy League society. Based on his own words, and his training as a historian, it appears that he was chosen by members of a secret network to write the real history of their rise to power. However, as Quigley later realized, these individuals did not expect or intend for him to publish their secrets for the rest of the world to see. Shortly after publishing *Tragedy and Hope* in 1966, "the Network" apparently made its displeasure known to Quigley's publisher, and the book he'd spent twenty years writing was pulled from the market. As Quigley recounts:

> The original edition published by Macmillan in 1966 sold about 8800 copies and sales were picking

---

2 *Wikipedia*, Carroll Quigley

up in 1968 when they "ran out of stock," as they told me (but in 1974, when I went after them with a lawyer, they told me that they had destroyed the plates in 1968). They lied to me for six years, telling me that they would re-print when they got 2000 orders, which could never happen because they told anyone who asked that it was out of print and would not be reprinted. They denied this until I sent them Xerox copies of such replies to libraries, at which they told me it was a clerk's error. In other words they lied to me but prevented me from regaining the publication rights by doing so. [Rights revert back to the copyright holder if the book is *out of print*, but not if the book is simply *out of stock*.]...Powerful influences in this country want me, or at least my work, suppressed.[3]

A Book like No Other

If you decide to read *Tragedy and Hope,* the first thing you're likely to notice is its size. At over thirteen hundred pages, approximately six hundred thousand words, and weighing in around five pounds, it's safe to say that it wasn't written for the casual reader. Nor was it written like a novel, bursting with scandalous and interesting conspiratorial tidbits on every page. Rather, as one would expect from an Ivy League historian, it is a long and often tedious read of which 95 percent consists of basic economic, political, and diplomatic history. However, within the other 5 percent, you'll find some truly astonishing admissions about the existence, nature, and effectiveness of covert power.

---

3 See "Letter to Peter Sutherland, December 9, 1975; reprinted in *Conspiracy Digest* (Summer 1976), and reprinted again in *American Opinion* (April 1983), page 29." Reference: En.wikipedia.org/wiki/Carroll_Quigley

In both *Tragedy and Hope* and *The Anglo-American Establishment,* Quigley reveals the existence of a secret network that formed to bring "all the habitable portions of the world" under its control.[4]

> **I know of the operations of this network because I have studied it for twenty years and was permitted for two years, in the early 1960's, to examine its papers and secret records**. I have no aversion to it or to most of its aims and have, for much of my life, been close to it and to many of its instruments. I have objected, both in the past and recently, to a few of its policies...but in general my chief difference of opinion is that **it wishes to remain unknown,** and I believe its role in history is significant enough to be known.[5]

Quigley informs us that this wealthy "Anglophile network" cooperates with *any* group that can help it achieve its goal.[6] (This includes Communists, which, on the surface, would seem to be the sworn enemy of super-wealthy capitalist conspirators.) He chronicles how the Network formed in the late 1800s in England and immediately began creating front groups. By 1919, it had formed the Royal Institute of International Affairs (also known as Chatham House), and it went on to create other extremely powerful institutes within "the chief British dominions and in the United States."[7] Hiding behind these front groups, the Network began secretly exercising its power.

In the United States the main institute was named the Council on Foreign Relations (CFR), which Quigley

---

4 *Tragedy and Hope,* page 131
5 *Tragedy and Hope,* page 950 (Throughout this book, unless otherwise noted, all **emphasis** in quoted text has been added.)
6 *Tragedy and Hope,* page 950
7 *Tragedy and Hope,* page 132

described as "a front for J. P. Morgan and company."[8]
Before long, the Network expanded its operations;
spreading like cancer into our universities, media, and
especially government "foreign policy."

On this basis, which was originally financial and
goes back to George Peabody,[9] there grew up in the
twentieth century a power structure between London and New York which penetrated deeply into
university life, the press, and the practice of foreign
policy. In England, the center was the Round Table
Group, while in the United States it was J. P. Morgan
and Company or its local branches in Boston, Phila-
delphia, and Cleveland.

The American branch of this "English Establish-
ment" exerted much of its influence through five
American newspapers (*The New York Times*, New York
Herald Tribune, *Christian Science Monitor*, the *Washing-
ton Post*, and the lamented *Boston Evening Transcript*).
In fact, the editor of the *Christian Science Monitor* was
the chief American correspondent (anonymously)…
It might be mentioned that the existence of this Wall
Street, Anglo-American axis is quite obvious once it
is pointed out.[10]

---

8 *Tragedy and Hope*, page 952
9 While we're on the topic of front groups, it's worth noting that Rothschild interests
likely used Morgan as a front *man*. In *The Secrets of the Federal Reserve*, Eustace Mullins
writes on page 49: "Soon after he arrived in London, George Peabody was surprised to
be summoned to an audience with the gruff Baron Nathan Mayer Rothschild. Without
mincing words, Rothschild revealed to Peabody, that much of the London aristocracy
openly disliked Rothschild and refused his invitations. He proposed that Peabody, a
man of modest means, be established as a lavish host whose entertainments would soon
be the talk of London. Rothschild would, of course, pay all the bills. Peabody accepted
the offer, and soon became known as the most popular host in London. It's hardly
surprising that the most popular host in London would also become a very successful
businessman, particularly with the House of Rothschild supporting him behind the
scenes." Quigley acknowledges that the Morgan firm originated as George Peabody
and Company (on pages 326 and 945 of *Tragedy and Hope*).
10 *Tragedy and Hope*, page 953

If the idea of powerful Wall Street insiders joining a secret foreign network to establish dominion over all "habitable portions of the world" and successfully penetrating "into university life, the press, and the practice of foreign policy" sounds like something you should have heard about, you're right. But the secret to why you haven't is contained in the story itself. (The successful "penetration" of universities, the press, and the government has proven quite useful to those who wish "to remain unknown.")

The Institute of Pacific Relations (IPR)

Quigley provides many examples of Network infiltration and manipulation. For instance, on pages 132 and 953 of *Tragedy and Hope,* he exposes yet another "front group" called the Institute of Pacific Relations (IPR). Because the IPR provides priceless insight into the deceptive nature and true power of the Network, we'll briefly cover it here. Let's begin with the final report of a US Senate investigation of the IPR. It stated, in part:

> The IPR has been considered by the American Communist Party and by Soviet officials as an instrument of Communist policy, propaganda and military intelligence. The IPR disseminated and sought to popularize false information including information originating from Soviet and Communist sources... **The IPR was a vehicle used by the Communists to orient American far eastern policies toward Communist objectives.**[11]

To the average person, it sounds crazy to suggest that a network of super-wealthy *capitalists* is secretly conspiring

---

11 http://en.wikipedia.org/wiki/Institute_of_Pacific_Relations

to gain control of the world. But it sounds even crazier to accuse these same super-wealthy capitalists of using their tremendous wealth and power to popularize a system of government (Communism) that would, in *theory* anyway, lead to the destruction of all their wealth and power. Surely, if such an unbelievable story were true, the free press would have shouted it from the rooftops...right? Wrong. Let's jump ahead for just a second and look at how Quigley described the Network-directed media cover up of the Senate investigation:

> It soon became clear that people of immense wealth would be unhappy if the investigation went too far and that the "most respected" newspapers in the country, closely allied with these men of wealth, would not get excited enough about any [revelations] to make the publicity worth while, in terms of votes or campaign contributions.[12]

As this demonstrates, the Network fully understands the importance of controlling public opinion. This also provides a glimpse into how it can do so. (If a disturbing truth isn't reported on by a "respected" news outlet, it might as well not exist. The vast majority of citizens will remain forever oblivious.) Additionally, in this particular case, any senator that insisted on taking the investigation "too far" would surely face a smear campaign by the same press that was ignoring the IPR story. Shortly thereafter, the "people of immense wealth" who ordered the smear campaign could be counted on to retaliate financially as well; by shifting all future campaign contributions to a more obedient candidate.

---

12 *Tragedy and Hope*, page 955

Needless to say, this type of *influence* can drastically affect how much attention an issue receives in the media. The merit and importance of a story will often take a backseat to the wishes of those who have the power to keep it quiet. More importantly, similar tactics of control can be applied in other areas as well. Keep that in mind as you read the following short summary of the IPR's activities, because the blueprint for directing perception and policies hasn't changed.

> In 1951 the Subcommittee on Internal Security of the Senate Judiciary Committee, the so-called McCarran Committee, sought to show that China had been lost to the Communists by the deliberate actions of a group of academic experts on the Far East and Communist fellow travelers whose work in that direction was controlled and coordinated by the Institute of Pacific Relations (IPR). **The influence of the Communists in IPR is well established, but the patronage of Wall Street is less well known.**
>
> The headquarters of the IPR and of the American Council of IPR were both in New York and were closely associated on an interlocking basis. Each spent about $2.5 million dollars [nearly $30 million when adjusted for inflation] over the quarter-century from 1925 to 1950, of which **about half, in each case, came from the Carnegie Foundation and the Rockefeller Foundation** (which were themselves interlocking groups controlled by an alliance of Morgan and Rockefeller interests in Wall Street). Much of the rest...came from firms closely allied to these two Wall Street interests, such as Standard Oil, International Telephone and Telegraph, International

General Electric, the National City Bank, and the Chase National Bank.[13]

On the Network's influence over Far East Policy:

> There is considerable truth in the...contention that the American experts on China were organized into a single interlocking group which had a general consensus of a Leftish character. It is also true that this group, from its control of funds, academic recommendations, and research or publication opportunities, **could favor persons who accepted the established consensus and could injure, financially or in professional advancement, persons who did not accept it.** It is also true that the established group, by its influence on book reviewing in *The New York Times*, the *Herald Tribune*, the *Saturday Review*, a few magazines, including the "liberal weeklies," and in the professional journals, **could advance or hamper any specialist's career. It is also true that these things were done in the United States in regard to the Far East by the Institute of Pacific Relations, that this organization had been infiltrated by Communists, and by Communist sympathizers, and that much of this group's influence arose from its access to and control over the flow of funds from financial foundations to scholarly activities.**[14]
>
> Awards for work in the Far Eastern area required approval or recommendation from members of IPR. Moreover, access to publication and recommendations to academic positions in the handful of great American universities concerned with the Far East required similar sponsorship. And, finally,

---

13 *Tragedy and Hope*, page 946
14 *Tragedy and Hope*, page 935

there can be little doubt that consultant jobs on Far Eastern matters in the State Department or other government agencies were largely restricted to IPR-approved people. The individuals who published, who had money, found jobs, were consulted, and who were appointed intermittently to government missions were those who were tolerant of the IPR line.[15]

Amazingly, after admitting all of this, Quigley somehow concludes:

The charges...accepted and proliferated by the neo-isolationists in the 1950's and by the radical Right in the 1960's, that China was "lost" because of this group, or that the members of this group were disloyal to the United States, or engaged in espionage, or were participants in a conscious plot, or that the whole group was controlled by Soviet agents or even by Communists, is not true.[16]

In Quigley's defense, the last part of his statement is obviously accurate: the group wasn't controlled by "Soviet agents or even Communists." Rather, according to Quigley himself, the group was controlled by a secret network of individuals who "have no aversion to cooperating with the Communists, or any other groups, and frequently does so."[17] But does this fact somehow exonerate them from a charge of "disloyalty"? Does it change the nature of their "conscious plot" to fabricate "consensus" on US policy toward China? Does it lessen their impact on the ultimate fate of China? No.

15 *Tragedy and Hope*, page 947
16 *Tragedy and Hope*, page 935
17 *Tragedy and Hope*, page 950

This is one of many cases where Quigley expresses a clear bias toward the Network and its *instruments*. Clearly, this bias clouds his judgment. For instance, he repeatedly describes the Network's methodical deception of others, but apparently he never questions whether he too might have been deceived. He describes the carnage of their "mistaken" policies, but their *good intentions* are always accepted without a second thought.

Combine this favorable bias with his open contempt for "the radical Right" and "neo-isolationists," and poorly reasoned conclusions are nearly unavoidable. His casual dismissal of the IPR's role in the fate of China provides but one shining example. That Quigley can admit the IPR had tremendous financial and political power, a specific agenda, and actually *achieved* its goals, but then attribute the rise of Mao Zedong solely to the "incompetence and corruption" of Chiang Kai-shek's regime is difficult to explain.[18]

Side Note: It's worth mentioning that shortly after the creation of the IPR in 1925 the civil war in China conveniently began. One possible reason (conjecture) for why the Network might have preferred a Communist regime in China is found in the following statement:

> From the broadest point of view the situation was this: The rivalry between the two super-Powers [the United States and Soviet Union] could be balanced and its tensions reduced only by the coming into existence of another Great Power on the land mass of Eurasia. There were three possibilities of this: a federated and prosperous Western Europe, India, or China. The first was essential; one of the others was highly desirable; and possibly all three might be

---

18 *Tragedy and Hope*, page 935

achievable**, but in no case was it essential, or even desirable, for the new Great Power to be allied with the United States.**

If the Soviet Union were boxed in by the allies of the United States, it would feel threatened by the United States, and would seek security by more intensive exploitation of its resources in a military direction, with a natural increase in world tension. If, on the other hand, the Soviet Union were boxed in by at least two great neutral Powers, it could be kept from extensive expansion by (1) the initial strength of such great Powers and (2) the possibility that these Powers would ally with the United States if the Soviet Union put pressure on them.[19]

The "Great Game" of playing one side off another, engaging in balance-of-power politics, is discussed many times throughout Quigley's book. I've included the reference above only because it provides a potentially logical motive (at least logical in the Realpolitik sense of the word) for the Network's policy toward China.

Now, returning to Quigley's characterization of the IPR scandal and the subsequent lack of media coverage referenced earlier: As a result of continuing pressure, spurred on by the "radical Right," the Network soon found itself the target of two Congressional investigations. Quigley describes the second of these investigations, the Reece Committee, this way:

A congressional committee, following backward to their source the threads which led from admitted Communists like Whittaker Chambers, through Alger Hiss, and the Carnegie Endowment to

---

19 *Tragedy and Hope*, page 1048

Thomas Lamont and the Morgan Bank, fell into the whole complicated network of the interlocking tax-exempt foundations. The Eighty-third Congress in July 1953 set up a Special Committee to Investigate Tax-Exempt Foundations with Representative B. Carroll Reece, of Tennessee, as chairman. It soon became clear that people of immense wealth would be unhappy if the investigation went too far and that the "most respected" newspapers in the country, closely allied with these men of wealth, would not get excited enough about any [revelations] to make the publicity worth while, in terms of votes or campaign contributions. An interesting report showing the Left-wing associations of the interlocking nexus of tax-exempt foundations was issued in 1954 rather quietly. Four years later, the Reece committee's general counsel, Rene A. Wormser, wrote a shocked, but not shocking, book on the subject called *Foundations: Their Power and Influence.*[20]

Quigley closes this chapter on the Network with the following:

The financial circles of London and those of the eastern United States...reflects **one of the most powerful influences in the twentieth-century American and world history**. The two ends of this English-speaking axis have sometimes been called, perhaps facetiously, the English and American Establishments. There is, however, a considerable degree of truth behind the joke, a truth which reflects a **very real power structure**. It is this power structure which the Radical Right

---

in the United States has been attacking for years in the belief that they are attacking the Communists.[21]

Again, as Quigley points out, the power structure that he exposed isn't loyal to Communism, or Socialism, or Fascism, or capitalism. The Network is happy to exploit the rhetoric of *any* movement or ideology, prop up any dictator or tyrant, and support any economic or political model, provided it serves their one overarching aim. That aim, to bring "all the habitable portions of the world under *their* control," is as old as the lust for power itself. The death and suffering that their policies have already caused in pursuit of this aim are incalculable. Allowing them to continue as they have will only bring more of the same. As W. Cleon Skousen states in *The Naked Capitalist*:

> As I see it, the great contribution which Dr. Carroll Quigley unintentionally made by writing *Tragedy and Hope* was to help the ordinary American realize the utter contempt which the network leaders have for ordinary people. Human beings are treated *en masse* as helpless puppets on an international chess board where giants of economic and political power subject them to wars, revolution, civil strife, confiscation, subversion, indoctrination, manipulation and deception.

Skousen hit the nail on the head. *Tragedy and Hope* revealed something even more important than "one of the most powerful influences in the twentieth-century American and world history." It inadvertently revealed the *mind-set* of those who wield such power. It exposed the astonishing arrogance and hypocrisy of those who feel they have the right to rule billions of other human beings.

---

21 *Tragedy and Hope*, page 956

If there is one goal for this book, it is to expose the attitude and inherent nature of those who seek to dominate others. Don't worry about remembering all of the dates and names that have been listed. Don't worry about trying to recall all of the specific events. (All of that information will always be here if you need to find it again.) Instead, make it a point to simply verify the following: there is no lie that these men will not tell. There is no crime that they will not commit. The only measure of "right" and "wrong," in their view, is whether their tactics succeed or fail. This might sound like hyperbole now, but by the end of this short book you will understand the truth of this assertion. (The Network's game is won by those who calculate properly, and *moral* considerations only impede accurate calculation.)

An Introduction to Realpolitik

Henry Kissinger personifies the essence of the Network mind-set. In his book *Diplomacy,* he introduces his readers to the amoral concepts of *raison d'état* (translated as "reasons of state," or state interests) and *Realpolitik.* The basis of both concepts, Kissinger explains, is that individual *men* can be judged negatively on moral grounds, but governments cannot. When it comes to government action, the only suitable judgment is based on whether or not the government achieves its ends.[22] Throughout his book, Kissinger praises those who are wise enough to govern by these concepts and practically mocks those who object on so-called "moral" grounds.

In praise of Cardinal de Richelieu (a seventeenth-century French statesman), Kissinger writes:

> Though privately religious, [Richelieu] viewed his duties as minister in entirely secular terms. Salvation

---

22 Henry Kissinger, *Diplomacy*, pages 34, 58, 103 +

might be his personal objective, but to Richelieu, the statesman, it was irrelevant. "Man is immortal, his salvation is hereafter," he once said. "The state has no immortality, its salvation is now or never." In other words, states do not receive credit in any world for doing what is right; they are only rewarded for being strong enough to do what is necessary.[23]

As the King's First Minister, [Richelieu] subsumed both religion and morality to *raison d'état*, his guiding light.[24]

Richelieu was indeed the manipulator described, and did use religion [as a tool of manipulation]. He would no doubt have replied that he had merely analyzed the world as it was, much as Machiavelli had. Like Machiavelli, he might well have preferred a world of more refined moral sensibilities, but he was convinced that history would judge his statesmanship by how well he had used the conditions and the factors he was given to work with.[25]

To clarify, according to statesman like Kissinger, the moral and legislative laws that limit the actions of ordinary men do not apply to a select few. To escape accountability, the ruling class needs only to invoke the name of the state. This, of course, is the same position held by past rulers who justified theft, deceit, torture, slavery, and slaughter *in the name of God*. The tactic has simply been modernized. Our new rulers have substituted "the state" for God. And conveniently for them, they *are* the state...and not just any state; they are the emerging, omnipotent, *global* state.

---

23 *Diplomacy*, page 61
24 *Diplomacy*, page 64
25 *Diplomacy*, page 65

Though citizens have been conditioned to believe that their statesmen and government instruments are in place to serve *them*, nothing could be further from the truth. Both the instruments and statesmen are part of an institutional apparatus that exists for the benefit of those who control it. Put another way: the *state* is nothing more than a collection of men and women who direct the resources and policies of government. Contrary to popular belief, it is an *institution* that exists for its own sake, to ensure its own "salvation," and to prevent the rise of anything that might challenge its power.

This is a harsh reality, and some will surely object on the grounds that the modern state is different. After all, it is built on the consent of the people. Democratic elections enable citizens to vote for who their leaders will be. They can choose from Republicans or Democrats. They can throw either out of office if they break their campaign promises.

But what if our so-called representative government is all a carefully crafted illusion? What if the Network *chooses* the candidates that we get to vote for? What if the Network's "experts," not the figureheads placed in official positions of power, are the ones who ultimately determine government policy? What if both political parties, right and left, are controlled by the exact same people? Quigley shines some light on this topic as well:

> The argument that the two parties should represent opposed ideals and policies, one, perhaps, of the Right and the other of the Left, is a foolish idea acceptable only to doctrinaire and academic thinkers. Instead, **the two parties should be almost identical, so that the American people can "throw the**

rascals out" at any election without leading to any profound or extensive shifts in policy.[26]

Quigley goes even further when describing the system that's now emerging:

> It is increasingly clear that, in the twentieth century, **the expert will replace...the democratic voter in control of the political system...Hopefully, the elements of choice and freedom may survive for the ordinary individual** in that he may be free to make a choice between two opposing political groups (even if these groups have little policy choice within the parameters of policy established by the experts)...**in general, his freedom and choice will be controlled within very narrow alternatives.**[27]

Does that statement alarm you? Let's hope so.

Facing Reality

Using Quigley's work as a starting point, this book will highlight how a small group of dominant men were able to secure control of local, national, continental, and even global policy. Though the power of this network is not complete, they are moving inexorably in that direction. Without increased awareness (and resistance), their unelected and unaccountable global state will become a reality. And though the illusion of national sovereignty might be maintained, the freedom of the world's citizens "will be controlled within very narrow alternatives."

---

26 *Tragedy and Hope*, page 1247
27 *Tragedy and Hope*, page 866

Before moving on to the next chapter, here are some of the key insights that we will cover in this book:

- *Real* power is unelected. Politicians change, but the power structure does not. The Network operates behind the scenes, for its own benefit, without ever consulting those who are affected by its decisions.

- The Network is composed of individuals who *prefer* anonymity. They are "satisfied to possess the reality rather than the appearance of power."[28] This approach of secretly exercising power is common throughout history because it protects the conspirators from the consequences of their actions.

- A primary tactic for directing public opinion and "government" policy is to place willing servants in leadership positions of trusted institutions (media, universities, government, foundations, etc.). If there is ever a major backlash against a given policy, the servant can be replaced. This leaves both the institution and the individuals who actually direct its power unharmed.

- Historically, those who establish sophisticated systems of domination are not only highly intelligent; they are supremely deceptive and ruthless. They completely ignore the ethical barriers that govern a normal human being's behavior. They do not believe that the moral and legislative laws, which others are expected to abide by, apply to them. This gives them an enormous advantage over the masses that cannot easily imagine their mind-set.

---

28 Quigley, *The Anglo-American Establishment*, page 4

- Advances in technology have enabled modern rulers to dominate larger and larger areas of the globe.[29] As a result, the *substance* of national sovereignty has already been destroyed, and whatever remains of its shell is being dismantled as quickly as possible. The new system they're building (which they themselves refer to as a *New World Order*), will trade the existing illusion of democratically directed government for their long-sought, "expert-directed," authoritarian technocracy.[30]

To be sure, it's difficult to accept these statements upon first hearing them. They challenge our world view and force us to reconsider everything that we've been taught to believe. It's much easier to dismiss these facts without further investigation; it's easier to accept comforting lies that alleviate our anxieties. But this, of course, is exactly the opposite of what must be done. If we allow ourselves to be manipulated, we empower the Network at our own expense.

Edward Bernays, perhaps more than anyone, helped establish the modern system of public manipulation. Drawing on the psychoanalytical techniques of his uncle, Sigmund Freud, Bernays became known as the father of propaganda.[31] His low opinion of the masses is best expressed in his own words. The following quotes are taken from his book *Propaganda*:

> No serious sociologist any longer believes that the voice of the people expresses any divine or specially wise and lofty idea. The voice of the people expresses the mind of the people, and that mind is made up for it by the group leaders...and by

---

29 *Tragedy and Hope*, page 1206
30 *Tragedy and Hope*, pages 866, 1200, 1201
31 *Wikipedia*, Edward Bernays

those persons who understand the manipulation of public opinion.

If we understand the mechanism and motives of the group mind, is it not possible to control and regiment the masses according to our will without their knowing about it?

Whatever attitude one chooses toward this condition...we are dominated by the small number of persons who understand the mental processes of the masses. It is they who pull the wires which control the public mind and contrive new ways to guide the world.

Political campaigns today are all sideshows... A presidential candidate may be "drafted" in response to "overwhelming popular demand," but it is well known that his name may be decided upon by half a dozen men sitting around a table in a hotel room.

The conscious manipulation of the masses is an important element in democratic society. Those who manipulate this unseen mechanism of society constitute an invisible government which is the true ruling power of our country.

Bertrand Russell, historian, philosopher, mathematician, cofounder of analytic philosophy,[32] and expert on the scientific method of human manipulation, describes a global "society of experts" this way:

The society of experts will control propaganda and education. It will teach loyalty to the world government, and make nationalism high treason. The government, being an oligarchy, will instill submissiveness

---

32 *Wikipedia*, Bertrand Russell

into the great bulk of the population...It is possible that **it may invent ingenious ways of concealing its own power, leaving the forms of democracy intact, and allowing the plutocrats or politicians to imagine that they are cleverly controlling these forms...whatever the outward forms may be, all real power will come to be concentrated in the hands of those who understand the art of scientific manipulation.**[33]

Purveyors of the *democratic* illusion assure us that sophisticated conspiracies and powerful *secret societies* exist only in the mind of paranoids and extremists. Their assurances are a lie. With Quigley as our guide, we'll trace the origins and operations of the Network that, by "concealing its own power," seeks to secretly dominate our world.

---

33 *The Scientific Outlook*, page 175

CHAPTER 2
Power Behind the Throne

As already mentioned, Quigley wasn't your run-of-the-mill historian. Unlike most respected academics, he wasn't afraid to talk about secret *conspirators* exercising power from the shadows. Nor was he afraid to point out that constitutions, parliaments, presidents, and emperors can all be used as a distraction, to divert attention away from the *real* ruling power behind the throne. As just one example, at about 190 pages into *Tragedy and Hope*, Quigley sets the record straight regarding the so-called Meiji Restoration in Japan.

By all outward appearances, the Restoration wrested power away from the shogun and placed it back in the hands of the Japanese emperor. But while this story of the emperor's return to power was spread far and wide, the reality of the situation was quite different. In truth, the *Restoration* had simply shifted power away from the shogun and into the hands of feudal lords who "proceeded to rule Japan in the emperor's name and from the emperor's shadow."[1]

> These leaders, organized in a shadowy group known as the Meiji oligarchy, had obtained complete domination of Japan by 1889. **To cover this fact with camouflage**, they unleashed a vigorous propaganda [of]

---

1 *Tragedy and Hope*, page 194

abject submission to the emperor which culminated
in the extreme emperor worship of 1941–1945.

To provide an administrative basis for their
rule, the oligarchy created an extensive govern-
mental bureaucracy...To provide an economic
basis for their rule, this oligarchy used their political influence to pay themselves extensive pensions
and government grants [and engaged] in corrupt
business relationships with their allies in the commercial classes...To provide a military basis for
their rule, the oligarchy created a new imperial
army and navy and penetrated the upper ranks
of these so that they were able to dominate these
forces as they dominated the civil bureaucracy. To
provide a social basis for their rule, the oligarchy
created...five ranks of nobility recruited from their
own members and supporters.

Having thus assured their dominant position...
the oligarchy in 1889 drew up a constitution which
would assure, and yet conceal, their political domination of the country.[2]

The oligarchy presented the constitution as "an emis-
sion from the emperor, setting up a system in which all government would be in his name, and all officials would be
personally responsible to him."[3] This seemingly legitimate
constitution called for a legislative body composed of both
an elected House of Representatives and a House of Peers.
Though these provisions were enacted, they were essentially
meaningless:

The form and functioning of the constitution was of
little significance, for the country continued to be

2 *Tragedy and Hope*, page 195
3 *Tragedy and Hope*, page 195

run by the Meiji oligarchy through their domination of the army and navy, the bureaucracy, economic and social life, and the opinion-forming agencies such as education and religion.[4]

Like *all* ruling classes, the Meiji maintained control by indoctrinating the masses in an ideology that served the oligarchs' interests. Specifically, they propagated the Shinto ideology, which called for subordination to the emperor. "In this system, there was no place for individualism, self-interest, human liberties, or civil rights."[5]

The Japanese people accepted this Shinto ideology, and as a result the Meiji oligarchy was able to ruthlessly exploit them in the emperor's name. However, interestingly enough, the Meiji were beholden to an even greater power. Behind them there existed yet another group, numbering no more than a dozen men, which represented the ultimate ruling power in Japan. Quigley explains:

> These leaders came in time to form a formal, if extralegal, group known as the *Genro*...Of this group, Robert Reischauer wrote in 1938: "It is these men who have been the real power behind the Throne. It became customary for their opinion to be asked and, more important still, to be followed in all matters of great significance to the welfare of the state. No Premier was ever appointed except from the recommendation of these men who became known as the *Genro*. Until 1922 no important domestic legislation, no important foreign treaty escaped their perusal and sanction before it was signed by the Emperor. These men, in their time, were the actual rulers of Japan."[6]

---

4 *Tragedy and Hope*, page 196
5 *Tragedy and Hope*, pages 197–198
6 *Tragedy and Hope*, page 200

The Nature of Secret Coercive Power

There is a very logical reason why coercive power prefers secrecy and deception: if the goal is to exploit and dominate others (without suffering the natural consequences of doing so), then transparency and honesty are not an option. As such, the basic *template* of coercive power (often hidden, always deceptive, and exercised in the name of something other than itself) is common throughout history. If "the name of God" is beyond reproach, then intelligent rulers will exercise their power in the name of God. If invoking the name of *democracy*, or the *state*, or the *emperor* will empower them, they will act in the name of any of these. This *is* the unchanging characteristic of those who effectively rule the masses: they will *say* and *do* anything to establish a system that serves their interests.

Stated another way: *morality* will never stop an individual or group that's willing to lie, steal, intimidate, imprison, torture, or kill in pursuit of their aims. Likewise, a piece of paper with words written on it (a constitution) and an easily manipulated democratic form of government will not stop them either. This latter point is particularly relevant today because the "opinion-forming agencies" have done everything in their power to convince us otherwise.

From a very early age, we are conditioned to believe that a constitution and democratic elections somehow prove that *we* are in control; that those who would seek illegitimate power over our lives cannot succeed with these protections in place. We are never asked to question whether this belief is actually *true*. We are never provided examples that might suggest that it is not true. For instance, did Stalinist Russia's constitution and elections of "democratic appearance and form"[7] protect the

---

7 *Tragedy and Hope*, page 392

people of Russia? Did a government that was "democratic in form"[8] prevent the rise of Hitler in Germany? Is the "Democratic People's Republic" of North Korea, with its regular elections, a true republic? Were the Genro unable to rule Japan as a result of the Japanese constitution and *elections*? Moving a bit closer to home, what about the **guaranteed** protections outlined in the constitution of the United States? Are these written protections sufficient to block the predations of an illegitimate ruling class? If you think they are, consider the following:

Today, in the "freest nation on earth," US representatives have claimed the authority to spy on US citizens without a warrant. This clearly violates the US Constitution. They have claimed the authority to arrest citizens and hold them forever without charges and without the right to challenge the legitimacy of their detention. This too violates the US Constitution. They have even claimed the authority to *kill* US citizens based on nothing more than an accusation... no judge, no jury, no public presentation of evidence or requirement to prove guilt.[9] This is an egregious violation of the individual protections outlined in the US Constitution.

Since US citizens never granted their representatives the authority to violate these legal restrictions on government power, these powers must have been seized. *Rulers* seize power; *representatives* do not. As noted in chapter 1, Quigley referred to these rulers as the "experts" who will replace "the democratic voter in control of the political system."

Here is where arguments about the inevitable destruction of national sovereignty really take root. In the eyes of the *experts*, it is merely a matter of time before one superior group of rulers finally achieves what all prior rulers have attempted (sufficient power to *compel obedience* over all areas

---

8 *Tragedy and Hope,* page 409
9 Search "National Defense Authorization Act" (NDAA) for more information.

of the globe). Quigley explains the progression of global coercive power this way:

> The increasing offensive power of the Western weapons systems has made it possible to compel obedience over wider and wider areas and over larger numbers of peoples. Accordingly, political organizations (such as the state)…have become larger in size and fewer in numbers…In this way, the political development of Europe over the last millennium has seen thousands of feudal areas coalesce into hundreds of principalities, and these into scores of dynastic monarchies, and, finally, into a dozen or more national states. The national state, its size measured in hundreds of miles [was possible only because it could] apply force over hundreds of miles.
>
> As the technology of weapons, transportation, communications, and propaganda continued to develop, it became possible to compel obedience over areas measured in thousands (rather than hundreds) of miles and thus over distances greater than those occupied by existing linguistic and cultural groups. It thus became necessary to appeal for allegiance to the state on grounds wider than nationalism. This gave rise, in the 1930's and 1940's, to the idea of continental blocs and the ideological state (replacing the national state).[10]

The consolidation that Quigley describes is more than a collection of historical facts. It captures the immutable nature of coercive power. Unchecked, rulers will *always* consolidate and centralize their control until there is nothing left for them to seize. And, unfortunately, this applies to human freedom as well as geographic resources: "One step leads to another, and

---

10 *Tragedy and Hope*, page 1206

every acquisition obtained to protect an earlier acquisition requires a new advance at a later date to protect it."[11]

So, accepting this reality, we wind up with a handful of important questions: Who are the rulers? To what extent can they "compel obedience" without meaningful resistance? How did they seize power? How do they maintain and expand their power? What are their unpunished crimes (past and present)? Most importantly, what are the strategic targets that we must strike to destroy their illegitimate rule? In the following chapters, we'll cover all of this and more. But first, we must begin at the beginning.

The Birthplace of a Network

Nearly one thousand years ago, a university was founded in England. Nearly one thousand years later, not only does that same university still exist, but it is ranked number one in the United Kingdom and consistently ranks among the top ten universities in the world.[12]

As one of the most prestigious institutions of higher learning, specializing in politics, the psychological sciences, and business, Oxford has a very long and distinguished history. It has produced dozens of prime ministers. It has produced archbishops, saints, famous economists like Adam Smith, and famous writers like R.R. Tolkien (*Lord of the Rings*) and Aldous Huxley (*Brave New World*) as well as philosophers like Thomas Hobbs and John Locke. Oxford also produced, approximately one hundred and fifty years ago, the progenitors of *the Network*. Let's flash back to this time in history, circa 1860.

Two opposing forces in the British Empire are clashing heads. On one side, many are arguing that the empire is immoral, expensive, and unnecessary. This argument, championed by men like William Gladstone, is eroding

---

11 *Tragedy and Hope*, page 133
12 *Wikipedia*, Oxford University

support for Britain's imperial policies. On the other side of the argument stands Benjamin Disraeli. Disraeli, a close ally of the queen, is a harsh critic of Gladstone and other "Little Englanders" who dare to challenge the benefits and necessity of the empire. Having referred to Gladstone as "God's only mistake," the intense rivalry between Disraeli and Gladstone is legendary. The following provides one example of their many disagreements:

> Disraeli and Gladstone clashed over Britain's Balkan policy...Disraeli believed in upholding Britain's greatness through a tough, "no nonsense" foreign policy that put Britain's interests above the "moral law" that advocated emancipation of small nations. Gladstone, however, saw the issue in moral terms: the Turks had massacred Bulgarian Christians and Gladstone therefore believed it was immoral to support the Ottoman Empire.[13]

Because Gladstone's moral arguments were gaining ground, a new institute was formed to counter the rising tide of anti-imperialism. Quigley writes:

> The Royal Colonial Institute was founded in 1868 to fight the "Little England" idea; Disraeli as prime minister (1874–1880) dramatized the profit and glamour of empire by such acts as the purchase of control of the Suez Canal and by granting Queen Victoria the title of Empress of India; after 1870 it became increasingly evident that, however expensive colonies might be to a government, they could be fantastically profitable to individuals and companies supported by such governments.[14]

13 http://en.wikipedia.org/wiki/Benjamin_Disraeli
14 *Tragedy and Hope*, page 129

And so, to protect the profits of Britain's imperial policies, the rhetoric used to justify imperialism slowly began to change. One man, appointed to a newly created professorship at Oxford, led the charge in teaching Oxford undergraduates the "new imperialism."

> The new imperialism after 1870 was quite different in tone from that which the Little Englanders had opposed earlier. The chief changes were that it was justified on grounds of moral duty and of social reform and not, as earlier, on grounds of missionary activity and material advantage. The man most responsible for this change was John Ruskin.
>
> Ruskin spoke to the Oxford undergraduates as members of the privileged, ruling class. He told them that they were the possessors of a magnificent tradition of education, beauty, rule of law, freedom, decency and self-discipline but that this tradition could not be saved, and did not deserve to be saved, unless it could be extended to the lower classes in England itself and to the non-English masses throughout the world. If this precious tradition were not extended to these two great majorities, the minority of upper-class Englishmen would ultimately be submerged by these majorities and the tradition lost.[15]

Based on these new justifications, the same immoral policies of conquest and subjugation found new support. The empire was now not only a matter of moral duty; it was a matter of self-preservation. (If the ruling elite failed to expand the empire, their civilized way of life would be lost to the unwashed masses.) It was a powerful message, and it had a "sensational impact" on one of Ruskin's students.

---

15 *Tragedy and Hope,* page 130

The student was so moved that he copied Ruskin's lecture word for word and kept it with him for thirty years.[16] He also, with a handful of other Ruskin devotees, went on to establish and fund the Network that Quigley referred to as "one of the most important historical facts of the twentieth century."[17] The student's name was Cecil Rhodes.

If you've heard of Cecil Rhodes, odds are it hasn't been within the context of him being "that guy who created a secret society to control the world." However, you may have heard of the Rhodes Scholarships at Oxford (or maybe the term *Rhodes Scholar*, a title given to students who studied under his program).[18] Maybe you've heard of the African nation of Rhodesia, or Rhodes University located in South Africa, both named after Rhodes. If you've ever bought a diamond, perhaps you've heard of the De Beers diamond company (a South African diamond monopoly, established by Rhodes).

Each of these stands as a testament to the extraordinary life and influence of Cecil Rhodes. But the most significant thing Rhodes established during his lifetime doesn't bear his name and remains almost completely unknown. This despite the fact that the secret society he founded in 1891,[19] and its subsequent "instruments," continues to operate to this day.

Building the Network

Rhodes extracted much of the original funding for his secret society from the diamond and gold mines of South Africa. After monopolizing these industries, the enormous

---

16 *Tragedy and Hope*, page 130
17 *The Anglo-American Establishment*, page ix
18 In *The Anglo-American Establishment*, page 33, Quigley writes: "The scholarships were merely a façade to conceal the secret society, or, more accurately, they were to be one of the instruments by which the members of the secret society could carry out its purpose."
19 *Tragedy and Hope*, page 131

wealth and influence that he secured enabled him to steadily increase the Network's reach. Quigley explains:

> Rhodes feverishly exploited the diamond and gold-fields of South Africa, rose to be Prime Minister of the Cape Colony (1890–1896), contributed money to political parties, controlled parliamentary seats both in England and in South Africa, and sought to win a strip of British territory across Africa from the Cape of Good Hope to Egypt.[20]

Not surprisingly, Rhodes didn't feel any moral conflict about his imperial desires or the methods that he used to attain them. He viewed himself as superior to those he intended to subjugate. In his last will and testament, he wrote:

> I contend that we are the finest race in the world and that the more of the world we inhabit the better it is for the human race. Just fancy those parts that are at present inhabited by the most despicable specimens of human beings what an alteration there would be if they were brought under Anglo-Saxon influence.[21]

A PBS series titled *Queen Victoria's Empire* credits Rhodes with inspiring a burst of "imperialistic fervor" in Britain. Near the end of the piece, it says of Rhodes:

> Cecil John Rhodes...became the greatest empire builder of his generation. To fund his dreams of conquest, he embarked on a ruthless pursuit of diamonds, gold and power that made him the most formidable and the most hated man in Africa.

---

20 *Tragedy and Hope,* page 130
21 http://en.wikipedia.org/wiki/Cecil_Rhodes

But this story is much bigger than the effect Cecil Rhodes had on Africa or British Imperialism over a century ago. Obviously, to properly tell the story of the Network, a handful of important individuals like Rhodes *do* need to be mentioned. However, to be clear, these individuals are not the main focus of this story. Instead, our focus will fall mainly on the instruments that Rhodes and his followers created or infiltrated, as well as the tactics they employed to secretly further their goals. (As powerful as any one individual might have been or currently is within the Network, the *instruments* and *tactics* are where the real power lies. Men eventually die; instruments and tactics can live on indefinitely.)

Side Note: If you *are* interested in a methodical and mind-numbing breakdown of all the individuals Quigley looked into while researching the Network (names, dates, titles, government positions, relationships to other powerful people, etc.), *The Anglo-American Establishment* provides pages and pages of text like this:

> Of Lord Salisbury's five sons, the oldest (now fourth Marquess of Salisbury), was in almost every Conservative government from 1900 to 1929. He had four children, of whom two married into the Cavendish family. Of these, a daughter, Lady Mary Cecil, married in 1917 the Marquess of Hartington, later tenth Duke of Devonshire; the older son, Viscount Cranborne, married Lady Elizabeth Cavendish, niece of the ninth Duke of Devonshire. The younger son, Lord David Cecil, a well-known writer of biographical works, was for years a Fellow of Wadham and for the last decade has been a Fellow of New College. The other daughter, Lady Beatrice Cecil, married W. G. A. OrmsbyGore (now Lord Harlech), who became a member of the Milner

TRAGEDY AND HOPE 101

Group. It should perhaps be mentioned that Viscount Cranborne was in the House of Commons from 1929 to 1941 and has been in the House of Lords since. He was Under Secretary for Foreign Affairs in 1935–1938, resigned in protest at the Munich agreement, but returned to office in 1940 as Paymaster General (1940), Secretary of State for Dominion Affairs (1940–1942), and Colonial Secretary (1942). He was later Lord Privy Seal (1942–1943), Secretary for Dominion Affairs again (1943–1945), and Leader of the Conservative Party in the House of Lords (1943–1945).[22]

Fortunately for you and me, there will be no such lists in this book.

The Network's First Instrument and
Some of Its Accomplishments

The first instrument created by Rhodes and his associates was the secret society itself. After seventeen years of planning,[23] Rhodes called a meeting and formally established the society. Inspired by the Jesuits,[24] the Illuminati,[25] and the Freemasons (of which he was a member),[26] Rhodes hoped to succeed where the other secret societies had failed. Using a "rings within rings" structure, the center ring of power (composed of Rhodes and just three other individuals) would control all of the outer rings. Of the three individuals

---

22 *The Anglo-American Establishment*, page 16
23 *The Anglo-American Establishment*, page 3
24 *The Anglo-American Establishment*, page 34
25 Ed Griffin, the Quigley Formula, http://www.republicmagazine.com/bonus-articles/griffin.html
26 Wikipedia, Cecil Rhodes

who shared the inner ring with Rhodes, Alfred Milner (later awarded the title *Lord* Milner) became the strongest.

> The goals which Rhodes and Milner sought and the methods by which they hoped to achieve them were so similar by 1902 that the two are almost indistinguishable. Both sought to unite the world...in a federal structure around Britain. Both felt that this goal could best be achieved by a secret band of men united to one another by devotion to the common cause...Both felt that this band should pursue its goal **by secret political and economic influence behind the scenes and by the control of journalistic, educational, and propaganda agencies.**
>
> With the death of Rhodes in 1902, Milner obtained control of Rhodes's money and was able to use it to lubricate the workings of his propaganda machine. This is exactly as Rhodes had wanted and had intended. Milner was Rhodes's heir, and both men knew it...In 1898...Rhodes said, "I support Milner absolutely without reserve. If he says peace, I say peace; if he says war, I say war. Whatever happens, I say ditto to Milner."[27]

Always on the lookout for potential helpers, Milner recruited mainly from Oxford and Toynbee Hall. He used his influence to place the new recruits into positions of power.

> Through his influence these men were able to win influential posts in government and international finance and became the dominant influence in British imperial and foreign affairs...Under Milner in South Africa they were known as Milner's Kindergarten until 1910. In 1909–1913 they organized semisecret

---

27 *The Anglo-American Establishment*, page 49

groups, known as Round Table Groups, in the chief British dependencies and the United States.[28]

As already covered in chapter 1:

> In 1919 they founded the Royal Institute of International Affairs (Chatham House)...Similar Institutes of International Affairs were established in the chief British dominions and in the United States (where it is known as the Council on Foreign Relations) in the period 1919–1927. After 1925 a somewhat similar structure of organizations, known as the Institute of Pacific Relations [IPR] was set up.[29]

The Anglo-American Establishment describes the Network's basic system of recruitment and placement this way:

> The inner circle of this group, because of its close contact with Oxford and with All Souls, was in a position to notice able young undergraduates at Oxford. These were admitted to All Souls and at once given opportunities in public life and in writing or teaching, to test their abilities and loyalty to the ideals of the Milner Group. If they passed both of these tests, they were gradually admitted to the Milner Group's great fiefs such as the Royal Institute of International Affairs, *The Times*, *The Round Table*, or, on the larger scene, to the ranks of the Foreign or Colonial Offices.[30]

This system proved to be very effective. It allowed the growing Network to remain hidden, while its founders

---

28 *Tragedy and Hope*, page 132
29 *Tragedy and Hope*, page 132
30 *The Anglo-American Establishment*, page 91

exercised a level of control that can "hardly be exaggerated." As proof, Quigley provides a partial list of the group's so-called accomplishments. Among them:

- The Second Boer War (1899–1902)
- The partitioning of Ireland, Palestine, and India
- Formation and management of the League of Nations
- British "appeasement" policy (empowerment policy) of Hitler
- Control of *The Times*, Oxford, and those who write "the history of British Imperial and foreign policy"

Quigley goes on to say:

> It would be expected that a Group which could number among its achievements such accomplishments as these would be a familiar subject for discussion among students of history…In this case, the expectation is not realized.[31]

Something else that is "not realized" when dispassionately rattling off a list of "accomplishments" like those above is the true gravity and life-altering impact of those events. To provide a little perspective, we'll briefly cover one of the aforementioned accomplishments here. They say a picture is worth a thousand words, so let's start with a picture of just *one* of the thousands of children (Lizzie Van Zyl) who starved to death in British concentration camps during the Second Boer War.

---

31 *The Anglo-American Establishment*, page 5

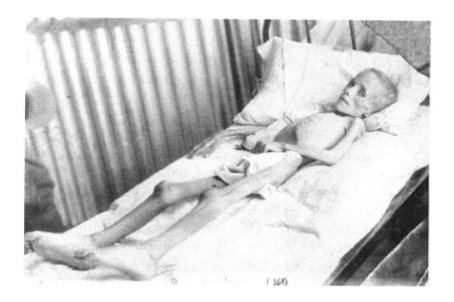

The Second Boer War

Rhodes, as a member of "the finest race in the world," needed money to fund his global-domination project. To obtain that money, he had no problem seizing valuable resources from the "despicable specimens of human beings" that it rightfully belonged to. As such, he used his dominant influence over British Imperial policy (the ability to direct British military force) against the Boers in South Africa.

It should be noted that his first attempt to grab Boer land and resources, a conspiracy known as the Jameson Raid, failed miserably. And though he and his Network had clearly directed the conspiracy and though the leaders he selected to overthrow the Boer government were caught in the act, the consequences of the attempted coup weren't sufficient to prevent a more ambitious conspiracy (the Second Boer War) that followed a few years later.

Side Note: Cecil's brother, Frank Rhodes, was among the leaders who were captured and tried by the Boer government for the Jameson Raid.[32] If there are any doubts about the benefits of being among the ruling class, this should settle the issue:

> For conspiring with Dr. Jameson...members of the Reform Committee...were tried in the Transvaal courts and found guilty of high treason. The four leaders were sentenced to death by hanging, but this sentence was next day commuted to 15 years' imprisonment; and in June 1896 [six months later] the other members of the Committee were released on payment of £2,000 each in fines, all of which were paid by Cecil Rhodes.
>
> Jan C. Smuts wrote in 1906, "The Jameson Raid was the real declaration of war...And that is so in spite of the four years of truce that followed...[the] aggressors consolidated their alliance...the defenders on the other hand silently and grimly prepared for the inevitable."[33]

In the years following the failed Jameson Raid, the Network began agitating for British annexation of the Boer Republics. After a sufficient British military buildup and failed negotiations, the inevitable finally came. Paul Kruger (known as the "face of Boer resistance"[34]) saw that war was unavoidable and issued a final ultimatum to the British, demanding that they withdraw all troops from the borders of the Transvaal Republic and the Orange Free State within

32 *Wikipedia*, Jameson Raid
33 http://en.wikipedia.org/wiki/Second_Boer_War
34 *Wikipedia*, Paul Kruger

forty-eight hours.[35] If the British refused, the two republics would declare war.

> Outrage and laughter were the main responses. The editor of *The Times* laughed out loud when he read it, saying "an official document is seldom amusing and useful yet this was both." *The Times* denounced the ultimatum as an "extravagant farce." *The Globe* denounced this "trumpery little state." Most editorials were similar to the *Daily Telegraph*, which declared: "of course there can only be one answer to this grotesque challenge. Kruger has asked for war and war he must have!"[36]

And war they did have, with all of the injustice and brutality that one should expect: theft, subjugation, suffering, and murder. Though the Network and its supporters expected a fast and easy victory over the "trumpery little" states that dared to challenge the British Empire, such was not the case. The Boers were skilled hunters and competent fighters. As weeks turned into months, and months turned into years, the Boers (determined to regain the independence of their own territory) drove the British to employ a scorched-earth policy.

> As British troops swept the countryside, they systematically destroyed crops, burned homesteads and farms, poisoned wells, and interned Boer and African women, children and workers in concentration camps.

---

35 It's worth noting that Jan Smuts was President Kruger's main political advisor and that *Smuts* wrote the ultimatum that made war inevitable. Why is this important? Because Smuts was also a "vigorous supporter of Rhodes" and eventually became "one of the most important members" of the Network. In other words, the Network had its agents play both sides of the conflict, carefully guiding the British and South African nations to war (*Tragedy and Hope*, page 137).

36 http://en.wikipedia.org/wiki/Second_Boer_War

The Boer War concentration camp system was the first time that a whole nation had been systematically targeted, and the first in which some whole regions had been depopulated.

Although most black Africans were not considered by the British to be hostile, many tens of thousands were also forcibly removed from Boer areas and also placed in concentration camps.[37]

Ultimately, the concentration camp system proved more deadly than the battlefield. By war's end, nearly 50 percent of all Boer children under sixteen years of age had "died of starvation, disease and exposure in the concentration camps." All told, approximately 25 percent of the Boer inmate population died, and total civilian deaths in the camps (mostly women and children) reached twenty-six thousand. (The picture of Lizzie Van Zyl represents just one of those twenty-six thousand faces.)[38]

Sadly, these numbers account for only Boer civilians killed. In all, the death toll of the Second Boer War exceeded seventy thousand lives, with more than twenty-five thousand combatants killed and an additional twenty thousand black Africans, 75 percent of whom died in the British concentration camps. But, of course, this was only just the beginning and a small price to pay for the Network. The defeated republics were absorbed into the empire and were eventually folded into the Union of South Africa (also a creation of the Network, which served as a British ally during the two World Wars).[39]

Hopefully, this short outline of the Second Boer War adds some depth to one of the early "accomplishments" of Rhodes and his fellow conspirators. Factor in the immeasurable suffering of some of their other so-called

37 *Wikipedia,* Second Boer War
38 *Wikipedia,* Second Boer War
39 *Wikipedia,* Second Boer War

accomplishments, like the million or so who died when they decided to partition India, or the millions more who died as a result of their Hitler-empowerment project, and Quigley's assertion that this group is "one of the most important facts of the twentieth century" is hard to deny.

As the British government suffered the political consequences of the Network's decisions, and as the British citizenry and soldiers paid the costs in blood and treasure, the secret society that Rhodes created was able to operate without fear of direct repercussions. The British government was now one of its instruments. Oxford, *The Times*, the League of Nations, and the Royal Institute for International Affairs (to name a few) were also its instruments. On the surface, each of these appeared unconnected. Beneath the surface, each was dominated by the same group of individuals.

In a rare moment of honest criticism, Quigley warns his readers:

> No country that values its safety should allow what the Milner Group accomplished in Britain—that is, that a small number of men should be able to wield such power in administration and politics, should be given almost complete control over the publication of the documents relating to their actions, should be able to exercise such influence over the avenues of information that create public opinion.
>
> Such power, whatever the goals at which it may be directed, is too much to be entrusted safely to any group.[40]

Building on that foundation, it's time now to shift away from the Network's impact on Europe, Africa, and Asia.

---

40 *The Anglo-American Establishment,* page 197

As interesting and tragic as those stories might be, there is another continent (North America) that Rhodes intended to control from the start.

In his first will, Rhodes resolved to create a global power so great that it would "render wars impossible." (More accurately, he should have stated: "Render *resistance* to the Network impossible.") Not surprisingly, this goal to create an unconquerable global power required "the ultimate recovery of the United States of America as an integral part of the British Empire."[41]

In the following chapter, we'll cover how the Network successfully infiltrated the political and economic system of the United States and turned it into just another one of its instruments in the quest for global domination.

---

41 *The Anglo-American Establishment,* page 33

CHAPTER 3

The Network "Recovers" America

Two men, Cecil Rhodes and Lord Milner, played an indispensable role in the creation and expansion of the Network. Their actions changed the world forever, and for that reason no depiction of the Network (or modern history for that matter) would be complete without mentioning their names.

Likewise, two additional men played an indispensable role in helping the Network achieve one of its crucial goals: regaining control of the United States of America. The first man, Edward Mandell House, was clearly a willing and deceptive servant. The second man, President Woodrow Wilson, was almost certainly a well-meaning dupe. But before bringing these two additional characters into the story, let's touch on *why* it was necessary for the Network to "recover" the United States and destroy its political and economic sovereignty.

Global Domination 101

There is always one nonnegotiable element in any plan to secure global domination: sovereign nations (truly *independent* nations) cannot be tolerated. Why? Because global domination is about centralizing all power into the would-be rulers' hands. Independent nations impede this consolidation and disturb the proper chain of command.

This seems straightforward enough, but, since it's rarely boiled down to its simplest form, it's worth repeating: to rule the world, **you must first destroy national sovereignty**. You must consolidate and control the *real* levers of power, regardless of the different *forms* of government that appear in each country.

If "democratic forms" of government can persuade the majority to accept your global policies, then democratic forms should be used. If tyrannical forms of government are more effective at gaining compliance, then let there be tyranny. If shifting from one form of government to another (turning nations and societies on their head) provides an opportunity to obtain your objectives; so be it. All that truly matters is that *you* control the *leaders* who appear to hold power and that you can contain or destroy those leaders if they forget (or simply haven't realized) who the real master is.

This is what Quigley meant when he said the Network's members are "satisfied to possess the reality rather than the appearance of power."[1] To the extent that they direct the political and economic machinery of nations, and to the extent they can destroy national sovereignty and impose *their* policies on the citizens of the world, they possess the *reality* of power. Accordingly, anything that weakens national sovereignty is their ally; anything that strengthens it is their enemy.

Unfortunately, as Ed Griffin points out in *The Quigley Formula,* many people struggle to believe that their highly respected "leaders" are conspiring to cheat them out of truly representative government. After all, our leaders constantly sing the praises of representative government. They

---

1 *The Anglo-American Establishment,* page 4

tell us that the citizens are sovereign, *voters* control national policies, and any suggestion to the contrary is ridiculous. After a lifetime of being fed this version of reality, the idea of a global conspiracy to destroy national sovereignty (involving both government and government advisors) is, understandably, difficult to accept. But the greatest weapon against knee-jerk disbelief often comes directly from the conspirators themselves. For instance, Arnold J. Toynbee (a high-ranking member of the Network), left little doubt when he wrote:

> I will hereby repeat that we are at present working discreetly but with all of our might to wrest this mysterious political force called sovereignty out of the clutches of the local national states of our world. **And all the time we are denying with our lips** what we are doing with our hands.[2]

As Quigley discovered, the Council on Foreign Relations (CFR) is nothing more than a front group for the Network.[3] This being the case, its position on national sovereignty is predictable. Here are a few choice quotes from CFR members taken from *Dishonest Money: Financing the Road to Ruin*, page 69:

> "The house of world order will have to be built from the bottom up rather than from the top down... an end run around national sovereignty, **eroding it piece by piece**, will accomplish much more than the old-fashioned frontal assault."—CFR member Richard Gardner

---

2 Arnold J. Toynbee, writing in the November 1931 edition of *InternationalAffairs*, as quoted by G. Edward Griffin in *The Quigley Formula*, http://youtu.be/ynVqPnMQ2sI?t=42m33s
3 *Tragedy and Hope*, pages 952 and 955

> **"We shall have world government, whether or not we like it.** The question is only whether world government will be achieved by consent or by conquest."—CFR member James Paul Warburg
>
> "Some dilution...of the sovereignty system as it prevails in the world today must take place...to the immediate disadvantage of those nations which now possess the preponderance of power...**The United States must be prepared to make sacrifices...in setting up a world politico-economic order.**"—CFR member Foster Dulles

Admiral Chester Ward, a longtime CFR member who later became a harsh critic, summed up the prevailing goal of the CFR this way: "the submergence of US sovereignty and national independence into an all-powerful one-world government."

Again, this policy toward national sovereignty shouldn't come as a surprise. The CFR is simply a creation of the Network, and, as such, it *was created* to help the Network achieve its goals. And though the CFR is just one of many instruments in the Network's arsenal, it is among the most powerful. Even though CFR members constitute only about .0015 percent of the US population, they have held, and currently hold, an inexplicably high percentage of the most influential positions in our society.

> **Almost all** of America's leadership has come from this small group. That includes presidents and their advisors, cabinet members, ambassadors, board members of the Federal Reserve System, directors of the largest banks and investment houses, presidents of universities, and heads of metropolitan newspapers, news services, and TV networks.[4]

---

4 *The Creature from Jekyll Island*, page 110

Before moving on, it's worth mentioning one additional and extremely important reason why the Network sought to regain control of the United States: just as the British government became a powerful *instrument* in the Network's toolbox, the United States offered an even greater opportunity. By seizing control of US foreign policy, the Network could now access the untapped military, economic, and political resources of America. It could use those resources to continue what's best described as its sovereignty-destruction project. As an added bonus, it could chain the political consequences and inescapable debt to the United States. And that's exactly what it has done.

For instance, since it was founded in 1947, the CIA (a creation of the Network)[5] has been used to destabilize and topple dozens of uncooperative nations covertly[6] while the US military (controlled by policy makers that are dominated by the Network) has been used to topple dozens directly. Again, the costs and blowback accrue to the United States; the benefits go to the Network. True, the United States does enjoy the "benefit" of *appearing* supremely powerful, but this is only a cruel joke. When the Network is satisfied that all major obstacles to its unelected rule have been removed, it will be a simple matter to destroy the US dollar, "justifiably" cut off the flow of money and credit to the United States, and create the political incentive (*necessity*) for the United States to fully enter the new global system.

---

5 Former CFR President, Allen Dulles, is credited with bringing the CIA into existence (*The Secret History of the CIA*, Joseph Trento, page 44). Dulles went on to head the CIA, using it to overthrow governments and engage in other highly illegal and unethical operations that served the Network's interests (see *Wikipedia*, Allen Dulles).
6 See "Covert US Regime Change Actions" at JoePlummer.com/bonus-material

Obviously, none of the Network's actions to this point (and none of its future plans) would have been possible without first seizing the levers of power in the United States. So for now, let's return to the two men who made that possible.

A Willing and Deceptive Servant

An unattractive and physically average man stands, alone and depressed, beneath an oak tree at the prestigious West Point Military Academy. It's graduation day. In the distance, his peers (the Class of 1920) anxiously await their chance to lead the army and the free world into the twentieth century. The president of the United States, his secretary of defense, and other distinguished guests are in attendance to honor the occasion, and this adds to what most see as an already-intoxicating atmosphere. All are filled with excitement and a sense of purpose...all but the man who stands beneath the oak.

Unlike his peers, he has paid attention to the world around him. He has studied the insidious influence of unrestrained wealth tearing at the fabric of the nation. Even the army itself had become little more than a prostitute in recent decades, forced to serve the interests of those who'd accumulated riches "beyond all bounds of need."

He quietly dreams of a "much-to-be-desired state of society," built upon the tenets of "socialism as dreamed of by Karl Marx."[7] Our hero, a "masterly man of prodigious intellect," resolves to hasten "a revolutionary adjustment" of US society.[8] But before he can fix the republic, he must first destroy it. He must overthrow the government, declare himself dictator, and shred that "obsolete" and "vulgar" document on which the republic was founded

---

7 *Philip Dru: Administrator,* page 24
8 *Philip Dru: Administrator,* page 31

(the US Constitution.) He alone will decide the laws of the nation...He will ensure the "desires of the people" are better met.[9] (Unless, of course, some of the people *desire* to resist his edicts; there will be no representation for them. They will be put to death. Likewise, the exercise of free speech against the dictator's policies will not be tolerated.[10])

If you've been checking footnotes over the past few paragraphs, you've noticed multiple references to a book entitled *Phillip Dru: Administrator.* It's a novel, originally published anonymously in 1912. Why reference this novel, you ask? Because we can learn a great deal about the "willing and deceptive servant" (Edward Mandell House) from the book's anti-American message.

To briefly recap: *Phillip Dru: Administrator* is the tale of an "intellectually superior" man who conspires to overthrow the US government, assume dictatorial powers, and pave the way for "socialism as dreamed of by Karl Marx." Our good-hearted hero concludes, along with other characters in the book, that the people are simply incapable of deter-mining their own best interests. As such, "a revolutionary adjustment" of their government (whether they like it or not), is necessary. The hero and his fellow conspirators set out to remake the United States as they see fit, and succeed.

If you haven't already guessed, *Phillip Dru: Administra-tor* was written by none other than Edward Mandell House himself.[11] In the book, House argues that dictatorship is necessary because the rich and powerful have taken con-trol, and they're using their power against the poor and less fortunate. To understand how shamefully cynical this is, consider the fact that House's propaganda was meant

---

9 *Philip Dru: Administrator,* page 107
10 *Philip Dru: Administrator,* page 74
11 *Wikipedia,* Philip Dru: Administrator

to strengthen, not weaken, the same "rich and powerful" individuals that his book condemned.

Side Note: This is one of the most common tactics employed by the Network for manipulating public opinion. It will point to an injustice (often caused by the Network itself), whip up an emotional firestorm, and, at the peak of hysteria, offer a *solution* that furthers its own agenda.

Maybe this is why House published his novel anonymously. It would be pretty hard to hook readers with his fight-the-elite storyline if they knew the author was "one of the first 'kingmakers' in modern American politics."[12] In any event, the book is worth reading, not for its entertainment value (it isn't well written), but because it's a short read that provides many insights into how easily a handful of men can manipulate a *democratic* system of government. Some notable examples include:

- How a senator can *pretend* to represent the citizens who voted for him while actually representing the "special interests" that he was elected to fight (page 35)
- How kingmakers, before throwing their weight behind a candidate, ensure that the indebted candidate will choose "advisors" from the kingmaker's approved list (page 38)
- If a puppet official gets out of line, how to bring them back under control (have the press attack them and have other powerful government puppets do the same, page 46)
- How to use the regulatory power of government to collect tributes and funnel tax money into companies

---

12 As quoted in *To End All Wars: Woodrow Wilson and the Quest for a New World Order*, page 20

you choose. How to be "generous" with other people's money and use that *generosity* to strengthen your hold on political power (page 94)

The book even takes a few contemptuous shots at the electorate itself. For instance, when describing one of the major instruments that's used to manipulate elected officials, we learn that the press "can make or destroy a man's legislative and political career, and the weak and the vain and the men with shifty consciences, that **the people in their fatuous indifference elect to make their laws**, seldom fail to succumb to this subtle influence" (page 120).

As already mentioned, House himself was a kingmaker. His connections to the Network gave him the power to make or break aspiring politicians, and he exercised this power with great skill. Prior to turning his attention to the national stage, House is credited with helping four different candidates secure the governorship of Texas.[13] But of all the *kings* that House managed to make, none paid better dividends than Woodrow Wilson.

Carefully selected and manipulated, House used Wilson to create the two essential funding mechanisms for the Network's "revolutionary adjustment" of US society. More specifically: prior to the election of Woodrow Wilson, the Network did *not* possess the power to tax US citizens' income or control the nation's money supply. Wilson signed both of these powers into existence shortly after he took office. More than anything, this enabled House and the Network to turn the United States away from sovereignty and toward servitude.

Professor Thomas J. Knock provides this keen insight into the relevance of House's book, *Philip Dru: Administrator.*

---

13 *Wikipedia*, Edward M. House

Philip Dru deserves serious attention if only for the prophetic self-exposition of its author. Clearly, House's driving ambition in life was to influence the course of history. To an extent, he succeeded...He was right on the mark when he wrote: "I was like a disembodied spirit seeking a corporeal form. I found my opportunity in Woodrow Wilson."[14]

Woodrow Wilson, a Well-Meaning Dupe

Before the Network chooses a candidate for a particular job, that candidate must be carefully screened. This obviously isn't a problem for those who have intelligence agencies and other investigative resources at their disposal. A vast amount of personal information can be easily collected on *any* individual[15] and, if the individual looks promising, a recruiter (like Mandell House) will know exactly what buttons to push to entice and or manipulate the new recruit. To say that Wilson must have looked very promising to the Network would be a colossal understatement. He had demonstrated loyalty to the ideals of global government and socialism, as well as contempt for the US Constitution, long before House selected him[16] for the presidency.

In his book *To End All Wars: Woodrow Wilson and the Quest for a New World Order*, Thomas J. Knock (a supporter of Wilson) provides a detailed look into Wilson's mind. The

---

14 As quoted in *To End All Wars: Woodrow Wilson and the Quest for a New World Order*, page 21
15 In his book *NATO's Secret Armies*, Daniele Ganser references one of the CIA's "commandments" as it applies to recruiting an individual. "When the...candidate is to be considered and analyzed with regards to recruiting—use all possible...sources and means of control and check: police, schools, societies, work places, friends, relatives, neighbors, eaves dropping, house searches. There must be a continuous and long lasting surveillance of the candidate before recruitment." *NATO's Secret Armies*, page 186
16 As quoted in *The Creature from Jekyll Island*, page 240, footnote 1: "*The Columbia Encyclopedia* (Third Edition, 1962, p. 2334) says the Democratic Party nomination went to Wilson when William Jennings Bryan switched his support to him 'prompted by Edward M. House.'"

similarities between Wilson and the so-called hero in *Philip Dru: Administrator* are very disturbing. Assuming the Network sought to establish a centralized world government, they could have hardly found a better advocate than Woodrow Wilson.

As early as 1887, Wilson had written of a "confederation" of empires[17] and expressed his agreement with the central idea behind state socialism. That idea, he wrote, is that "no line can be drawn between private and public affairs which the State may not cross at will…it is very clear that in fundamental theory socialism and democracy are almost if not quite one and the same."[18]

In Wilson's opinion, the US government needed to move toward centralized socialist control and unlimited power in order to stop "the aggrandizement of giant corporations that threatened to swallow up, not only individuals and small businesses, but democratic government itself." Wilson went on to condemn "selfish, misguided individualism" and proclaimed "we ought all to regard ourselves as socialists." He saw that concentrated and unaccountable power had enabled "the rich and strong to combine against the poor and weak," and it was high time for government to "lay aside" timidity and "make itself an agency for social reform as well as political control."[19]

Each of these arguments is nearly identical to those offered by House's fictional hero. But unlike House (who used the arguments deceptively, to justify seizing greater power), Wilson probably believed that his solutions would weaken the monopolistic forces he spoke out against. And, if so, this made Wilson much more valuable to the Network than the typical insincere politician who'd say anything in

---

17 *To End All Wars: Woodrow Wilson and the Quest for a New World Order*, page 12
18 As quoted in *To End All Wars: Woodrow Wilson and the Quest for a New World Order*, page 7
19 As quoted in *To End All Wars: Woodrow Wilson and the Quest for a New World Order*, page 7

exchange for a paycheck and some power. Wilson would openly and *passionately* build for the Network what it could never openly build for itself.

But if these aspects of Wilson's personality and ideology were not enough, there was one final asset that the Network could exploit: Woodrow Wilson was a man of towering arrogance and hypocrisy. He had no aversion to the creation of imperial power, provided it was directed by the "right people" (like himself, no doubt) and provided it was used for the "right reasons" (to be determined by the same.) In the case of the United States, he stated, "I believe that God planted in us visions of liberty…that we are chosen…to show the way to the nations of the world how they shall walk in the paths of liberty."[20]

As with most politicians, when Wilson uses the pronoun "we" (as in "we are chosen"), he would have been more honest to use the pronoun "*I*." More to the point: he felt that God had chosen *him* to secure global liberty by force, and there is at least one reference, provided by Sigmund Freud, where Wilson drops all rhetorical subterfuge:

> God ordained that I should be the next President of the United States. Neither you nor any other mortal or mortals could have prevented it.[21]

Additional quotes further clarify the strength of Wilson's ego. For instance, in his confidential journal, he wrote: "Why may not the present generation write, through me, its political autobiography."[22] In an address he gave as president (July 4, 1914), Wilson proclaimed that the role of the United States was to be "the light which shall shine

---

20 As quoted in *To End All Wars: Woodrow Wilson and the Quest for a New World Order,* page 11
21 As quoted in *Woodrow Wilson, a Psychological Study,* page xi
22 As quoted in *Psychological Warfare and the New World Order,* page 52

unto all generations and guide the feet of mankind to the goal of justice and liberty and peace."[23] And to achieve this, Wilson generously pledged "every dollar" of America's wealth, "every drop of her blood," and all the "energy of her people."[24]

Even Henry Kissinger took aim at Wilson's "conceit":

> In Wilson's view, there was no essential difference between freedom for America and freedom for the world...he developed an extraordinary interpretation of what George Washington had really meant when he warned against foreign entanglements. Wilson redefined "foreign" in a way that would surely have astonished the first president. What Washington meant, according to Wilson, was that America must avoid becoming entangled in the *purposes* of others. But, Wilson argued, nothing that concerns humanity "can be foreign or indifferent to us." Hence America had an unlimited charter to involve itself abroad...what extraordinary conceit to derive a charter for global intervention from a Founding Father's injunction against foreign entanglements, and to elaborate a philosophy of neutrality that made involvement in war inevitable![25]

Wilson's desire to create a global power structure that "no nation" or "probable combination of nations" could resist,[26] coupled with his messiah complex, provided the perfect psychological ingredients for turning the man into

---

23 As quoted in *To End All Wars: Woodrow Wilson and the Quest for a New World Order*, page 20
24 *To End All Wars: Woodrow Wilson and the Quest for a New World Order*, page 96
25 *Diplomacy*, page 48
26 *To End All Wars: Woodrow Wilson and the Quest for a New World Order*, page 112

a useful idiot.[27] Servando Gonzales summed up the final equation perfectly: "Wilson was a man intoxicated with the sense of his own importance and historical relevance" and, as such, he could be "easily manipulated by a trained intelligence officer (like Edward Mandell House)."[28]

The evidence suggests that this is exactly what happened. The Network had no reason to reveal itself or its New World Order plans to Wilson. Rather, it had every reason to let him believe the crusade for global government was *his* idea, his divine purpose, to "make the world safe for democracy."

In his book, *The New Freedom*, Woodrow Wilson spoke out against a shadowy monopolistic power that was exercising undue influence in the United States. He wrote:

> Since I entered politics, I have chiefly had men's views confided to me privately. Some of the biggest men in the United States, in the field of commerce and manufacture, are afraid of somebody, are afraid of something. They know that there is a power somewhere so organized, so subtle, so watchful, so interlocked, so complete, so pervasive, that they had better not speak above their breath when they speak in condemnation of it.[29]

How ironic that this same "organized, watchful, and pervasive" power is what put Woodrow Wilson in the White House...and this brings us to another very important part of the story.

Assuming we accept the fact that Wilson was a dupe, cynically used by the Network to further its already-established

---

27 Wikipedia, "useful idiot": "In political jargon, *useful idiot* is a pejorative term for people perceived as propagandists for a cause whose goals they do not understand, and who are used cynically by the leaders of the cause."

28 *Psychological Warfare and the New World Order*, page 53

29 From Woodrow Wilson's book, *The New Freedom*

agenda, we still haven't addressed the most impressive swindle of all: that the Network successfully duped millions of Americans into electing him in the first place.

The Election Deception

Few voters ever stop to consider the way in which they initially meet "their" choices for president. If a strange man were to knock on their door and say "I'm running for president of the United States," there is almost zero chance they'd view him as a legitimate candidate. However, if they meet *the exact same stranger* through one of the Network's main propaganda instruments (radio, print, or television), suddenly the reaction is very different. Suddenly the stranger *deserves* a serious look.

This is what Bernays referred to as "one of the most firmly established principles of mass psychology," and the Network applies the principle masterfully. Essentially, it is this: the vast majority of people accept the idea that "*credible*" individuals and organizations should be trusted to do their reasoning *for* them.

In the case of elections, the public trusts the so-called credible media to narrow the field down to the top-tier candidates. A political "sideshow" ensues and, at the end, voters choose who they'd prefer to have in office. But their choice isn't what they perceive it to be. Sure, they *are* technically choosing who they prefer, but they are choosing from a list of candidates *that was chosen* for them.

Sadly, this sleight of hand works just as well today as it did one hundred years ago. And unless this concept becomes widely understood, it will work one hundred years from now as well. Returning to Bernays, from his book *Propaganda*:

Political campaigns today are all sideshows, all honors, all bombast, glitter, and speeches. These are for the most part unrelated to the main business of studying the public scientifically, of **supplying the public with party, candidate, platform…and selling the public these ideas and products.**

In short: without the Network's backing, a candidate will remain a relative nobody in the election. They will be relegated to begging door to door for enough money to run an (almost meaningless) advertising campaign. However, *with* Network backing, the candidate can count on millions of dollars in campaign donations, a long list of credible endorsements, and a nearly priceless amount of exposure through the Network's propaganda instruments. (In the unlikely event that a truly independent candidate emerges, with enough money or a large-enough following to gain some ground, the Network will simply use its instruments to smear and ostracize the candidate and the candidate's supporters.)

To be clear, this isn't to suggest that the Network-backed candidates are necessarily involved in the election deception. "President of the United States" is a job title that fewer than forty-five men have held. The desire to join the ranks of such an exclusive club, with all of its attendant perks, is undoubtedly very real. The candidates might even genuinely disagree with a few positions held by their opponents. In fact, it's even better if they do. (The meaningless bickering between them, and the partisan hysteria it incites among the public, only adds to the overall illusion of voter choice.) But on the issues that matter most to the Network, each sponsored candidate is virtually identical in value.

The beauty of this system is its simplicity. The Network scouts potential talent, performs the necessary background checks, and, after conveying its expectations, offers its vital assistance to a handful of candidates. After some "bombast, glitter, and speeches," the public chooses from the products (party, candidate, and platform) that were put before them.

Now, let's quickly expand a little on *how* and *why* the Network ousted incumbent president William Howard Taft and installed Woodrow Wilson.

Summary of the 1912 Coup

The 1912 election presented an incredible opportunity for the Network. Although William Howard Taft had served the conspirators well (by openly entertaining the idea of relinquishing US sovereignty and supporting the Network's long-sought funding mechanism, the income tax[30]), he'd failed to support the one measure that was more important than all others. He refused to support Nelson Aldrich's plan to hand the nation's money supply over to the Network through the creation of a central bank.[31] Since the central bank was necessary to truly dominate the United States, Taft's rejection of the Aldrich plan constituted a major transgression. But there was a remedy, and that remedy's name was Woodrow Wilson.

Wilson had done more than "openly entertain the idea of relinquishing national sovereignty," he'd developed a near-fanatical obsession with the idea. There would be no problem getting him to passionately evangelize the New World Order on behalf of the Network.

It would also be no problem getting Wilson to sign the Network's income-tax scam into law. (The income tax was sold as a way to punish the rich and enrich the poor. In reality, the tax simply extracts money from US citizens and dumps it directly into the Network's projects and pockets.)

30 *Wikipedia*, William Howard Taft
31 *The Creature from Jekyll Island*, page 451

Last but certainly not least, control of the nation's money supply would be far easier to secure with Wilson in the White House. For one reason, Wilson admitted that he really didn't understand central banking,[32] and this was *very* convenient. The Network could provide all the "right" advisors, steering the creation of the so-called Federal Reserve System from start to finish.

Another reason the central bank would be easier to secure under Wilson is because the entire issue had been successfully framed in partisan terms. That is, a previous central-bank plan had been put forward by a Republican senator named Nelson Aldrich. Since everyone knew that Aldrich was a Network-connected insider, the legislation was shot down by Democrats when it bore his name. (For this, the Democrats were largely seen as having protected the little guy from another big-business Republican scheme.)

With the people convinced that the Democrats had protected them, any alternative central-bank plan put forward under a Democratic administration would rouse far less suspicion. The Network could simply drop the name "Aldrich," wrap the legislation in some *progressive* rhetoric, and sell the exact same thing with Wilson and his Democratic administration acting as trusted pitchmen. (Like the income tax, the central bank would be presented as a way to "protect the people" from the rich and powerful. In truth, it accomplished the exact opposite.)

Side Note: The central-bank issue is so crucial to the Network's plan for dominating the world that I've written an entire book on the subject.[33] A sizable amount of the next chapter will be devoted to this topic, but, for now, here is

---

32 *The Creature from Jekyll Island,* page 459
33 See *Dishonest Money: Financing the Road to Ruin*

what Quigley said the Network intended to create with its central banking power:

> ...a world system of financial control in private hands able to **dominate the political system of each country**...The apex of the system was to be...**a private bank owned and controlled by the world's central banks which were themselves private corporations. Each central bank...sought to dominate its government** by its ability to control Treasury loans, to manipulate foreign exchanges, to influence the level of economic activity in the country, and to influence cooperative politicians by subsequent economic rewards in the business world.[34]

As a quick reminder, this isn't a case of Quigley *guessing* at the Network's intentions. He speaks with the authority of a man who, in his own words, *knows* "of the operations of this network" because he "studied it for twenty years and was permitted for two years, in the early 1960's, to examine its papers and secret records."[35]

So, when comparing the Republican candidate, Taft, to the Democratic candidate, Wilson, there was no question who the Network wanted more. The decision was made, Mandell House paid Wilson a visit, and the process of grooming Wilson for the presidency began.

> In November 1911, Wilson met Colonel Edward Mandell House, one of the first kingmakers in modern American politics. "Almost from the first," the Colonel later recalled, "our minds vibrated in

---

34 *Tragedy and Hope*, page 324
35 *Tragedy and Hope*, page 950

unison." Wilson concurred: "Mr. House is my second personality...His thoughts and mine are one."[36]

James Perloff describes a follow-up meeting at the Democratic Party headquarters in New York:

> Wilson received an "indoctrination course" from the leaders convened there, during which he agreed, in principle, to do the following if elected:
>
> - Support the projected Federal Reserve [central bank];
> - Support income tax;
> - Lend an ear to advice should war break out in Europe;
> - Lend an ear to advice on who should occupy his cabinet.[37]

As mentioned in footnote 16, House pulled all of the necessary strings to ensure the Democratic nomination for president went to Wilson. But as impressive as that level of influence might be, it's still a long way from actually putting a man in the White House. And, unfortunately for the Network, Taft was *heavily* favored to win against its preferred candidate. Not a problem.

As "luck" would have it, the Network found another potential candidate that it could run against Taft. Not just any candidate, mind you, but a former two-term Republican president. And not just any two-term Republican president, but the same one that Republican President Taft had just replaced in 1909: Teddy Roosevelt.

---

36 *To End All Wars: Woodrow Wilson and the Quest for a New World Order,* page 20
37 *The Shadows of Power—The Council on Foreign Relations and the American Decline,* page 27

This was a brilliant strategic move. The most obvious reason being, ten months prior to the 1912 election, Roosevelt had expressed a willingness to support the Aldrich plan.[38] Therefore, whether Wilson or Roosevelt won, the Network could get its central bank. But the most obvious reason isn't the only or best reason for why the Network poured more than ten million dollars[39] (inflation adjusted) into Roosevelt's campaign. Sure, Roosevelt was acceptable, but the Network still *preferred* Wilson. And by splitting the vote, they could have him. Perloff explains:

> Polls showed incumbent President Taft as a clear favorite over the stiff-looking professor from Princeton. So, **to divide the Republican vote**, the [Network] put money behind Teddy Roosevelt on the Progressive Party ticket. J.P. Morgan and Co. was the financial backbone of the Roosevelt campaign. The strategy succeeded. Republican ballots were split between Taft and Roosevelt, and Woodrow Wilson became President with only forty-two percent of the popular vote.[40]

The full results of the 1912 election were as follows: Wilson received 41.8 percent of the vote, Roosevelt received 27.4 percent, and Taft received only 23.2 percent.[41] How is that for impressive? William Howard Taft, a man who would have handily won the election with a strong majority, wound up dead last in a three-way race against two Network-manufactured candidates. House summed it up this

---

38 *The Creature from Jekyll Island*, page 455
39 *The Creature from Jekyll Island*, page 453
40 *The Shadows of Power—The Council on Foreign Relations and the American Decline*, page 27
41 *Wikipedia*, 1912 presidential campaign

way: "Wilson was elected by Teddy Roosevelt."[42] The rest, as they say, is history.

After the election, House proceeded to fill the president's important cabinet positions with the best advisors the Network had to offer. He guided Wilson's policy decisions like a "disembodied spirit" that had "found its opportunity" to shape the world with Wilson's hands.

Before the end of 1913, the income tax would be law. Before the end of 1913, the central bank would be a reality. These new instruments provided the funding and leverage that the Network needed to greatly accelerate its sovereignty-destruction project. But they, alone, would not provide the greatest opportunity to capitalize on Wilson's evangelical crusade to "make the world safe for democracy." Only a long and protracted world war, with funding guaranteed by the new instruments, could achieve that.

Once again, as luck would have it, just such an opportunity presented itself shortly after Wilson took office. World War I provided the political impetus for the Network's first major attempt at establishing a global government (the League of Nations). And although it wasn't as successful as they might have hoped, the League of Nations, along with all the other "instruments" that came into existence under Wilson, laid the foundation for all of the Network's progress over the past one hundred years.

---

42 As quoted in *The Creature from Jekyll Island*, page 456

CHAPTER 4
Money: The Ultimate Instrument

"Antiquity presents everywhere…the spectacle of a few
men molding mankind according to their whims, thanks
to the prestige of force and fraud."
—Frederic Bastiat[1]

Hopefully by now we've established the fact that a small,
powerful, and secretive group can alter the course of world
history. Additionally, we've established that this form of coercive power (hidden, dishonest, and dangerous) is nothing
new. It existed thousands of years ago, it existed hundreds
of years ago, and it exists today. Only the names, sophistication, and reach of the "instruments" have changed. Since
this form of power is inherently illegitimate, we need no
further justification to free ourselves from it.

   As noted, a handful of individuals have played such an
important role in the creation of our current system that
their names must be mentioned. However, targeting individuals within the system isn't going to solve our problems.
Even if only one out of one thousand people are genius-level sociopaths (the percentage is probably *much* higher),
that equals seven million potential recruits for the Network to draw from. In other words, there will always be an
inexhaustible pool of replacements available to fill the tiny

---

1 *The Law*, page 50

number of key policy-making posts within the system. For this reason, the predatory system *itself* must be destroyed.

Fortunately for us, there is a vital target for us to strike; one foundational element that the entire system is built on and cannot stand without: the Network's control of money. *This* is their primary weapon, and it is well within our power to take it from them.

The vast majority of people—people like you and me—don't think of money as a weapon. For us, it's simply something that we earn and then use to purchase products and services. The Network, on the other hand, has a much, *much* deeper understanding of what money is and how to wield its power. For them, money isn't about acquiring more material goods or services; it's about acquiring more *control* over the resources and instruments that govern human behavior. When viewed in this light, their seemingly insatiable desire to accumulate and control money makes more sense.

Keep in mind, this doesn't mean that personal ownership of money is the Network's most effective monetary weapon. In fact, we could take away the personal fortunes of all of its members and, if that's all we did, their power would remain undisturbed, and they would rebuild their fortunes in no time. This is because the Network knows something that most of us do not: *control* of money, not actual "ownership," is what truly matters. Where you and I cannot imagine having the ability to control money that doesn't belong to us, the Network cannot imagine having it any other way.

In this chapter, we'll cover the three primary mechanisms that the Network uses to perpetuate its monetary power. These mechanisms are: (1) the ability to combine and control the earnings of others, (2) the ability to directly confiscate the earnings of others, and (3) the ability to create money out of thin air.

1: Combine and Control Money

Beginning on pages 50–51 of *Tragedy and Hope*, Quigley speaks of a group that employs "financial capitalism" to monopolize business and control government. As experts in "financial manipulation," these men "aspired to establish dynasties of international bankers" and, according to Quigley, they succeeded at a level that rivaled the political dynasties of past centuries. Centered in London, with offshoots in New York and Paris, the power of this group is described as overwhelming in significance and "occult" in nature. By 1850[2] they could access the immense monetary power of "the Stock Exchange, the Bank of England, and the London money market." But this was just the beginning.

> In time, they brought into their financial network… commercial banks and savings banks, as well as insurance companies, to form all of these into a single financial system on an international scale which manipulated the quantity and flow of money.

Just to clarify: these men did not *own* the money that citizens placed in commercial and savings banks. They did not *own* the money that citizens paid into retirement funds, insurance funds, or trust funds. However, as already mentioned, they didn't need to own the money. All they needed was the power to *control* it, and *that* they had. As long as an institution within their "financial network" held the funds, they could direct those funds toward increasing

---

2 It's worth noting that this period of "financial capitalism" clearly predates the Rhodes-created network that Quigley describes in both *The Anglo-American Establishment* and *Tragedy and Hope*. As such, it's reasonable to suggest that the real roots of the Rhodes network (and the real power) existed long before Cecil Rhodes entered the picture. However, since this book focuses on the *proven* conspiracy (identified and exposed by Quigley), a detailed account of what existed before Rhodes will have to be told elsewhere.

their power. They, alone, determined how and where that
enormous, international pool of money would be invested.

> Bankers,   especially...international   investment
> bankers, were able to dominate both business and
> government. They could dominate business...
> because investment bankers had the ability to sup-
> ply, or refuse to supply, capital...they took seats on
> the boards of directors of industrial firms, as they
> had already done on commercial banks, saving
> banks, insurance firms and finance companies....
> **they funneled capital to enterprises which yielded
> control, and away from those who resisted.**[3]

Side Note: Quigley points out that bankers have far less
power over those who can finance their own operations.[4]
As such, any group seeking to create a ruling "dynasty of
international bankers" would be wise to create a system that
is built on debt and undermines independent financing.
Anything that devours or wipes out the wealth of outsiders
will create endless opportunities for members of the dynasty
who have an *inexhaustible*[5] supply of money to loan (always
with strings attached):

> The power of investment bankers over governments
> rests on a number of factors, of which the most signifi-
> cant, perhaps, is the need of governments to borrow
> money. Just as businessmen go to commercial banks
> for current capital advances...so a government has to
> go to merchant bankers (or institutions controlled
> by them) to tide over the shallow places caused by

3 *Tragedy and Hope*, pages 60 and 61
4 *Tragedy and Hope*, pages 56 and 60
5 These international bankers eventually gave themselves the power to simply create
money out of thin air, so they could then "loan it" to others.

irregular tax receipts. As experts in government bonds, the international bankers not only handled the necessary advances but provided advice to government officials and, on many occasions, placed their own members in official posts...

In addition to their power over government based on government financing and personal influence, bankers could steer governments in ways they wished them to go by other pressures. Since most government officials felt ignorant of finance, they sought advice from bankers whom they considered to be experts in the field. **The history of the last century shows...that the advice given to governments by bankers, like the advice they gave to industrialists, was consistently good for bankers, but was often disastrous for governments, businessmen, and the people generally**. Such advice could be enforced if necessary by manipulation of exchanges, gold flows, discount rates, and even levels of business activity.[6]

To summarize: using enormous amounts of other people's money, international bankers essentially purchased their way into powerful business and government positions. With each new position, they gained control of more money. With control of more money, they gained access to more positions (so on and so forth). Through this process they secured enough monetary power to *enforce* their "advice" on both businesses and governments alike, expanding the reach of their hidden dynasties each step of the way.

This now brings us to the Network's two crowning achievements of 1913: the federal income tax and the Federal Reserve System.

---

6 *Tragedy and Hope*, pages 61 and 62

Using *government* as its instrument, the Network granted itself the legal authority to both create and directly confiscate the money it needs to finance its global objectives. The enormity of this topic, especially regarding the legal right to *create* money, requires hundreds of pages to cover properly. This chapter will provide only a short introduction. To fully understand the power derived from creating money, I highly recommend further research into the Federal Reserve System.[7] For now, let's start with the easier of the two funding mechanisms: not money *creation*, but money *confiscation*.

2: Confiscate Money

On page 938 of *Tragedy and Hope*, Quigley draws a flawed conclusion. He assumes that J. P. Morgan, Rockefeller, Carnegie, etc., must have *lacked* control over the government in 1913. If they had more power, he suggests, they would have stopped the federal income tax from becoming law. Like so many others who've accepted the alleged purpose of the income tax, Quigley fails to put two and two together: an income tax that is paid into a system *that the Network controls* only serves to strengthen the Network's position. It creates another massive flow of other people's money to tap into.

Even if high-ranking members like J. P. Morgan, Rockefeller, Carnegie, etc., had paid the income tax like everyone else, they'd still gain control over far more money than they paid in. (The amount of money collected from the rest of the population *each year* ran into the billions by 1917, then the tens of billions by the mid-1940s, then the hundreds of billions by the mid-1970s, and it runs into the trillions today.)[8]

---

7 For a good beginner's guide (under two hundred pages) *read Dishonest Money: Financing the Road to Ruin.* For a much more thorough account (six hundred pages), I highly recommend *The Creature from Jekyll Island.*
8 USGovernmentRevenue.com

Remember, they don't have to *own* that money to determine how it's spent.

Of course, these men did not pay income taxes like everyone else. Instead, they used the government to establish "tax-exempt" foundations *before* the income tax became law. This not only enabled them to shield their own fortunes, but it also enabled them to gain further control over Ivy League education and the federal government itself. Remarkably, Quigley acknowledges the ultimate effect of the income tax and the tax-exempt foundations, but he doesn't seem to think about it much further:

> These tax laws drove the great private fortunes... into tax-exempt foundations which became a major link in the Establishment network between Wall Street, the Ivy League, and the Federal government.[9]

For insight into how the Network really felt about the income tax, we can simply turn our attention back to E. M. House. In his book *Philip Dru: Administrator* (written anonymously before the income-tax amendment was passed), House openly attacked the "grotesque" American Constitution because it prevented "the government" from collecting an income tax from its citizens.[10] Shortly after House's choice for president (Woodrow Wilson) was placed in office, the "grotesque" constitutional barrier was removed, and the money began to flow.

Sadly, few Americans realize that the United States did not have a permanent personal income tax prior to

9 *Tragedy and Hope*, page 938
10 *Philip Dru: Administrator*, page 107

1913.[11] Think about that for a minute...America went from being a sparsely settled nation of wilderness in 1776 to the most prosperous and arguably most powerful nation on the planet *without* an income tax. Contrary to the popular canard, a lack of income tax *does not* mean your country is doomed (socially, politically, militarily, and economically) to the global status of Somalia.

Here's another little-known fact about the income tax: if we abolished the personal income tax today, the federal government would still collect about $3 billion *per day* ($125 million per hour) in revenue. Compare that to its revenue in 1913 of less than $1 billion *per year,*[12] and the obscenity of what the Network has achieved becomes pretty clear. Even after adjusting for inflation, the numbers are still alarming. (One billion dollars per year in 1913 would equal about $25 billion per year today.[13] At the current rate of federal spending, that inflation-adjusted $25 billion would be gone in a little over two days!)[14]

All of this federal spending requires an ever-expanding river of money. Follow that river, and you'll find that it inevitably empties into an ocean of Network-connected industries and "interests." Even humanitarian "government" services like food stamps are handled by JP Morgan and generate millions of dollars for the firm. Start looking into the military-industrial complex, which serves the ultimate Network interest (its sovereignty-destruction project), and the costs, financial and otherwise, boggle the mind. But as bad as all of this is, we've still only scratched the surface.

---

11 A *temporary* income tax was imposed by Lincoln to fund the Civil War in 1861. Though the tax outlived the war, it ended circa 1873. An attempt in 1894 to create a *permanent* income tax was ruled unconstitutional by the Supreme Court a year later (see: Pollock v. Farmers' Loan & Trust Company). It wasn't until 1913, with the passage of the sixteenth amendment, that our current federal income tax came to be.

12 USGovernmentRevenue.com/classic

13 USInflationCalculator.com

14 USGovernmentRevenue.com/classic

Yes, the income tax essentially handed the Network a license to steal. Without its instrument (government), there would be no way to directly confiscate trillions of dollars annually from the labor of US citizens. The power of this funding mechanism, which did not exist for nearly 140 years of our nation's history, has strengthened the Network's global influence beyond measure. However, even on its best day, the so-called income tax runs a distant second to the greatest monetary power of all: the power to *create money* out of thin air.

3: Create Money—Create Credit—Create Inescapable DEBT

In the next chapter, we'll briefly cover the basic mechanics of creating money, credit, and inescapable debt. For now, let's cover something that's arguably more important and *definitely* easier to understand: the implications of possessing such incredible monetary power and the story of how the Network seized it. First, the implications. We'll start small and work our way up.

Can you imagine if the government gave you 100 million dollars? Think about that for a minute. Tomorrow, at noon, the government has agreed to transfer $100 million into your bank account, no strings attached…Got it? OK, let's go a little further.

Can you imagine if the government gave you 500 million dollars? How about $1 billion? Better yet, what if it simply decided to give you $1 *trillion?* It's difficult to get your mind around such large numbers, but really *try* to imagine what it would be like. For instance, if the government gave you $1 trillion and if you invested it, earning only a 7 percent annual return, you'd wind up with over $5.5 billion per month in additional income (roughly $192 million *per day.*)[15]Imagine having the ability to spend $192 million *per day* without ever depleting a penny of the $1 trillion you were given. How much power would you have? And with so much money to spend, how many individuals and institutions would want to be your friend?

Now, let's take it one step further...What if the government gave you *all* of the dollars? What if you were given the exclusive right to create every single dollar that exists? Try to get your head around *that* concept. (If a dollar exists anywhere in the world, it only exists because *you* were given the right to create it.) *Now* how much power do you have? The following quote provides a pretty good idea:

> "I am afraid the ordinary citizen will not like to be told that the banks can, and do, **create money**...And they who control the credit of the nation **direct the policy of Governments and hold in the hollow of their hands the destiny of the people.**"—Reginald McKenna, British Chancellor of the Exchequer, as quoted in *Tragedy and Hope*[16]

That statement is about as straightforward as it gets, and it comes from a man who had intimate knowledge of the topic. He worked at the highest levels within the system and is stating, unequivocally, exactly how it *is*. Those who create money and control the credit of the nation "direct the policy of governments and hold in the hollow of their hands the destiny of the people." So why is it, if *creating money* and controlling credit confer so much power, that so few people understand either of these topics? Shouldn't we

---

15 Seven percent of $1 trillion equals $70 billion per year. $192 million per day, times 365 days, equals $70,080 million (or, $70 billion and $80 million).
16 *Tragedy and Hope*, page 325

all be taught the dangers of such power? Is it any surprise that we aren't?

Again, Quigley provides some insight. He explains that, for the Network to achieve its objectives, "it was necessary to **conceal**, or even to **mislead**, both governments and people about the nature of money and its methods of operation."[17] This practice of deceiving governments and people about money continues to this day because it's the only way for the Network to maintain its current level of power. Rest assured, if the vast majority of people do not understand what central banks are or how they operate, it's because they were *not meant* to. Our global monetary system was created by men who "conceal" and "mislead" as a matter of course. It's not only how they conduct their business, it's how they intend to secure their "far-reaching aim," reiterated below.

> The powers of financial capitalism had a far-reaching aim, nothing less than to create **a world system of financial control...able to dominate the political system of each country and the economy of the world as a whole.** This system was to be controlled... by the **central banks** of the world acting in secret agreements...**Each central bank**, in the hands of men like Montagu Norman of the Bank of England [and] Benjamin Strong of the New York Federal Reserve...**sought to dominate its government** by its ability to control Treasury loans, to manipulate foreign exchanges, to influence the level of economic activity in the country, and to influence cooperative politicians by subsequent economic rewards in the business world. In each country **the power of the**

---

17 *Tragedy and Hope*, page 53

**central bank rested largely on its control of credit
and money supply.**[18]

It was, for this purpose, that the Network created the
Federal Reserve System.

The Federal Reserve System

In chapter 3, we covered President Taft's undoing: he
refused to support the Network's plan to create a central
bank in the United States. And since the Network couldn't
fully "dominate the political system" of the United States
without control of its "credit and money supply," Taft was
toppled and Wilson was installed. Shortly after taking
office, Wilson signed the Federal Reserve Act into law, and
the central bank was born.

However, this isn't the full story of how the Federal
Reserve System came to be. Just as citizens were misled into
believing that *they* chose Wilson in the 1912 election, they
were also misled into believing the Federal Reserve Act
was written to protect them from predatory international
bankers. The sad truth is, predatory international bankers
secretly wrote the legislation themselves and used government to turn their wishes into law.

This is a piece of the puzzle that Quigley seems to have
missed. He acknowledges that Network titans like Rockefeller and Morgan had enough power to cause a financial
panic whenever they chose. He admits that they used their
power to their own advantage, wrecking "individual corporations, at the expense of the holders of common stocks."
He even admits that J. P. Morgan precipitated the "panic of
1907."[19] But the fact that their power could have been used
to both take out competition *and* incite public demands for

18 *Tragedy and Hope*, page 324
19 *Tragedy and Hope*, page 72

"monetary reform" (*reform* that would be directed by the Network itself) is not covered. It's a glaring omission.

In short, the Network needed a central bank to "dominate the political system" of the United States, but it needed another crisis[20] to finally sell the scheme. With that perspective in mind, the panic of 1907 looks very different. First, J. P. Morgan *causes* the panic (which, to this day, is rarely mentioned), then he and Rockefeller *halt* the panic (for which, to this day, they're *still* portrayed as saviors), and out of the suffering and chaos, "public demands" for legislative intervention finally reach critical mass. "The government" then forms a monetary commission to investigate and solve the problem (headed by none other than Network insider and US senator, Nelson Aldrich), and the commission decides that a central bank is needed to solve the nation's woes. From there, it was simply a matter of writing the legislation and handing it off to the "right" politicians.

Of course, the Network had to conceal the fact that *it* would be writing the legislation itself, and this presented some problems. The lengths it went to in order to hide its role reads like a scene out of a James Bond novel.

---

20 The panics of 1873 and 1893 caused widespread suffering and stirred demands for monetary reform. Public opinion was already leaning heavily toward the need for legislative intervention, and the panic of 1907 provided the final push. If the idea that bankers would actually create a panic to serve their interests seems like a stretch, consider the case of Nicholas Biddle. As President Andrew Jackson was trying to shut down Biddle's 2nd Bank of the United States, the banker intentionally crashed the economy and blamed the ensuing financial crisis on Jackson. This served to turn public opinion *against* Jackson and in favor of the bank. Discussing the tactic, Biddle commented, "Nothing but widespread suffering will produce any effect on Congress...Our only safety is in pursuing a steady course of firm restriction...I have no doubt that such a course will ultimately lead to...recharter of the Bank." Referring to Jackson, Biddle remarked, "This worthy President thinks that because he has scalped Indians and imprisoned Judges, he is to have his way with the Bank. He is mistaken." (As quoted in *The Creature from Jekyll Island*, page 354)

> If you were alive in 1910, you wouldn't have been invited to the meeting...In fact, you would have never known that a meeting took place. Despite the enormous impact on your country's future, the scheme to create a new "monetary system" was none of your business.
>
> This is where the story of the Federal Reserve System begins. The banking empires of Rockefeller, Rothschild, Morgan and Warburg...sent [six] representatives on their behalf to the privately owned Jekyll Island off the coast of Georgia. To prevent the men from being recognized, the island's permanent employees were sent on vacation and carefully screened temps took their place. Each man was sworn to secrecy and instructed to only use their first name to further conceal their identity. (Nearly two decades passed before any of the conspirators publicly admitted they'd participated in the meeting.) In that meeting, the financial elite created for themselves the monetary system that we live under today.[21]

Had this meeting been covered in the press, the headline might have read: "POWERFUL BANKERS CONSPIRE ON PRIVATE ISLAND TO SEIZE MONETARY CONTROL." But then again, had it been covered in the press, the Federal Reserve Act would have never passed. Citizens wanted Congress to weaken the destructive powers of international banking interests, not expand them.

Unfortunately, the Jekyll Island story didn't leak until 1916[22], years after the damage had already been done. And even *after* it was exposed, "educators, commentators, and

---

21 *Dishonest Money: Financing the Road to Ruin*, pages 2 and 3
22 Reported by B. C. Forbes, who went on to found *Forbes* magazine; reference *Secrets of the Federal Reserve*, page 2

historians" continued to deny that the meeting ever took place.[23] Anyone who pointed out the nefarious origins and authors of the Federal Reserve Act was smeared and dismissed as a conspiracy theorist. Fortunately, the truth finally did come out, and the conspiracy theorists were vindicated. Perhaps the most definitive admission came from Frank A. Vanderlip, president of the most powerful New York bank at the time (National City Bank of New York, now Citibank):[24]

> There was an occasion near the close of 1910, when I was as secretive—indeed as furtive—as any conspirator...I do not feel it is any exaggeration to speak of our secret expedition to Jekyll Island as the occasion of the actual conception of what eventually became the Federal Reserve System...Discovery, we knew, simply must not happen, or else all our time and effort would be wasted. If it were to be exposed publicly that our particular group had got together and written a banking bill, that bill would have no chance whatever of passage by Congress... although the Aldrich Federal Reserve plan was defeated when it bore the name of Aldrich, nevertheless its essential points were all contained in the plan that finally was adopted.—Frank A. Vanderlip in the 1935 *Saturday Evening Post* article, "From Farm Boy to Financier"[25]

Despite this admission over seventy-five years ago, despite other participants and their biographers who've admitted the same, despite the fact that Federal Reserve Chairman (Ben Bernanke) returned to Jekyll Island in 2010

---

23 *The Creature from Jekyll Island*, page 8
24 http://en.wikipedia.org/wiki/Citibank
25 www.SaturdayEveningPost.com/2012/05/24/archives/banking.html

to commemorate the FED's founding one hundred years earlier[26]; still the vast majority of people have never heard of the trip to Jekyll Island and have *no idea* that "international bankers" created the system that was supposed to protect them from international bankers.

But again, should we be surprised? The education system and mainstream media are the two most powerful instruments for distributing information and creating mass awareness. Regarding the media, just a handful of global news corporations can, in one day, make *billions* of people around the world simultaneously aware of something that was completely unknown the day before. With this kind of power, the Network can choose to spread any lie, or withhold any truth, that it chooses. Then there is education: millions of students can be taught the real story behind the Federal Reserve System, or they can be taught the smokescreen of "government intervention to protect the public." They can be taught the dangers of centralized banking power, or they can be taught nothing at all. At the end of the day, if people aren't looking beyond the Network's instruments for their information, they cannot expect to know what the Network doesn't want them to know.

Even Quigley, apparently, was unaware of the trip to Jekyll Island. He makes no mention of the meeting in either *Tragedy and Hope* or *The Anglo-American Establishment.* Since he obviously had no aversion to exposing comparable duplicity, it's reasonable to assume he didn't know that particular part of the Fed's history. Or, perhaps he consulted some of the respected "educators and historians," who convinced him there was no evidence that it ever happened.

---

26 From the Federal Reserve Bank of Atlanta website, titled "A Return to Jekyll Island": "The conference was held to mark the centenary of the 1910 Jekyll Island meeting that resulted in draft legislation [the Aldrich Plan] for the creation of the U.S. central bank." http://www.frbatlanta.org/news/conferences/10jekyll_index.cfm

Whatever the reason, it's an unfortunate oversight. Nothing demonstrates the Network's power more convincingly than its ability to secretly write legislation that governs, or outright *creates*, its own instruments. And on that note...

With its legislation successfully written, Taft ousted, and Wilson in the White House, it would seem that the Network could rest easy. However, there was one more swindle needed to guarantee passage of the Federal Reserve Act. To help garner public support, the *very same* people who helped author the legislation on Jekyll Island began speaking out publicly *against* it.

> As the Federal Reserve Act moved closer to its birth...both Aldrich and Vanderlip threw themselves into a great public display of opposition. No opportunity was overlooked to make a statement to the press—or anyone else of public prominence—expressing their eternal animosity to this monstrous legislation...Since Aldrich was recognized as associated with the Morgan interests and Vanderlip was President of Rockefeller's National City Bank, the public was skillfully led to believe that the [big bankers were] mortally afraid of the proposed Federal Reserve Act. *The Nation* was the only prominent publication to point out that every one of the horrors described by Aldrich and Vanderlip could have been equally ascribed to the Aldrich Bill as well. But this lone voice was easily drowned by the great cacophony of deception and propaganda.[27]

The newly packaged Glass-Owen Federal Reserve Act, which mirrored Aldrich's version in "all essential provisions,"[28] was put forward by Democrats as being

27 *The Creature from Jekyll Island*, pages 463 and 464
28 *The Creature from Jekyll Island*, page 461

radically different; a bill written by selfless public servants to protect the citizenry from selfish, out-of-control banking interests. And as Vanderlip, Aldrich, and other "big-business Republicans" continued to attack the "new" legislation, more and more well-meaning Americans fell for the ruse.

> The voice of the people expresses the mind of the people, and that mind is made up for it by…those persons who understand the manipulation of public opinion…It is they who pull the wires which control the public mind and contrive new ways to guide the world.[29]

Meanwhile, as the citizens were being guided to the desired opinion publicly, Edward Mandell House ensured that Wilson and Congress were being properly guided privately. *The Intimate Papers of Col House* leave little doubt that he acted as the direct liaison between the Network and relevant politicians during the creation of the central bank. (House directed the politicians while Paul Warburg, the primary author of the Jekyll Island legislation, directed House.) Ed Griffin summarizes House's role this way:

> As far as the banking issue was concerned, Colonel House was the President of the United States, and all interested parties knew it. Wilson made no pretense at knowledge of banking theory. He said: "The greatest embarrassment of my political career has been that active duties seem to deprive me of time for careful investigation. I seem almost obligated to form conclusions from impressions instead of from study…I wish that I had more knowledge, more

---

29 Edward Bernays, *Propaganda*

thorough acquaintance, with the matters involved."
To which Charles Seymour adds: "Colonel House
was indefatigable in providing for the President the
knowledge that he sought…The Colonel was the
unseen guardian angel of the bill."[30]

Here is a perfect example of Quigley's observation:
ignorance of banking led politicians to trust the advice of
bankers and that this was "consistently good for bankers,
but was often disastrous for governments…and the people
generally." The great irony is that Quigley himself does not
seem to fully understand the nature of the banking system.
There are a few things in *Tragedy and Hope* that support this
conclusion; I'll cover them briefly.

First, on page 58, Quigley presents what he calls a "paradox" of banking practice: bankers prefer monetary deflation (a reduction in the money supply) because it *increases*
both the value of the money that they control and the interest rates that they can charge borrowers. However, he states
that they inevitably abandon the "deflationary idea" in
favor of inflating the money supply (which they accomplish
by issuing bank loans) because of their "eagerness to lend
money at interest."

To Quigley's credit, he acknowledges that bankers can
gain an extra form of *profit* from this supposed "conflict":
by increasing the money supply with loans, they increase
the indebtedness of others and drive prices up. Then, by
decreasing the money supply, they can force many debtors
into foreclosure and confiscate whatever collateral was
pledged to secure their loans. He also acknowledges that
this manipulation of the money supply was a "prominent
aspect" of the so-called "business cycle" and that it was
"destructive to business and industry."[31]

---

30 *The Creature from Jekyll Island*, page 459
31 *Tragedy and Hope*, pages 58 and 59

My question is: Where is the paradox?

If you're a member of the Network, this is a fundamental feature of the banking system that you've created. What better way to crush or control competitors in "business and industry"? You not only enjoy the normal benefits of controlling loans (loaning money only to those who yield control and withholding it from those who resist), but you also have a mechanism for trapping debtors and then seizing their assets. If you do decide to confiscate their collateral—rather than bury the borrower in additional debt with additional strings attached—you've effectively gained ownership of a real asset with money that you created out of thin air. (Remember, that's how our current banking system operates. When the Network wants to issue a loan, it pulls a check from its magic checkbook, writes in the loan amount, and *poof*—the money for the loan is created on the spot.)

Quigley states that too much deflation could sometimes be "disastrous" for the bankers because it forced "the value of the collateral below the amount of the loans it secured." Sorry, but even this claim needs addressed. An unpaid principal loan balance of say $100,000, secured by an asset that sells for only $80,000 (or less), does not necessarily equal a loss for the bank.[32] And if the goal is to drive a competitor into bankruptcy, then the math involving so-called "losses" gets even more interesting. What *appears* to be a loss on paper (due to a gap between the amount of principal owed on a loan and what is ultimately obtained during liquidation) can actually be viewed as a great investment. Sure, a

---

32 As a simple example, consider an interest-only loan on $100,000 at 6 percent interest. At the end of five years, the debtor defaults, and the asset is sold for only $80,000. In this case it looks like the bank has lost money (the debtor still owed $100,000, and the bank only recovered $80,000 from the sale of the asset). However, if you factor in the INTEREST payments that were made over five years ($30,000), you see that the bank actually walks away with a profit of $10,000 ($80,000 sale price + $30,000 in interest payments equal $110,000). In rare instances, the bankers might actually lose some of the dollars that they created out of thin air for a loan. When that happens, those "losses" tend to be turned to profits via "government" bailouts.

portion of the dollars (created out of thin air) are not fully repaid, but that "cost" is minor compared to what it would have cost to purchase the competitor outright. Add in the *dividends* of market consolidation, and the return on investment is simply *fantastic.*

Next, there is the issue of the gold standard. Here again, it seems that Quigley has fallen for a false narrative: in this case, that the gold standard was the most sophisticated mechanism of monetary control that the elite could devise. That *gold* (rather than the control of money and debt, which gold only facilitated) was the root of their monetary power. If these myths are accepted as true, then his assertion that bankers sincerely tried to "save the gold standard" makes perfect sense. However, a closer look at their actions (and the ways in which they benefited from those actions), leads to a more logical conclusion: it was far more profitable to destroy the gold standard than it was to preserve it. To create ever-increasing piles of money and debt out of thin air, the limitations of gold had to be removed.

On pages 256 and 257 of *Tragedy and Hope,* Quigley nearly stumbles into the truth. While discussing the beginning of World War I, he tells the story of military men and financial experts who believed the war would be over within six months. This prediction was based on the fact that gold reserves (used to pay for the expenses of war) would be depleted within that amount of time. However, by *suspending* the gold standard, the duration of the war (along with the enormous debts and banker profits associated with it), grew far beyond anything that a gold standard would have supported.

> All the Great Powers were on the gold standard under which...**paper money could be converted into gold on demand**. However, each country suspended the gold standard at the outbreak of war.

This removed the automatic limitation on the supply of paper money...each country proceeded to pay for the war by borrowing from the banks. The banks **created the money** which they lent by merely giving the government a deposit of any size against which the government could draw checks. **The banks were no longer limited in the amount of credit they could create because they no longer had to pay out gold for checks on demand**...the problem of public debt became steadily worse because governments were financing such a large part of their activities by bank credit.[33]

From this perspective, the advantages of permanently "suspending" the gold standard are self-evident. When a bank creates "paper money" loans that are backed by gold, it runs the risk of losing its gold reserves. When a bank creates paper money loans that are backed by *nothing*, then its gold reserves are perfectly safe. Additionally, without gold backing, there are no longer any firm limits on how many loans the banking system can create. Limits, if any, are determined by the wishes of those who control the system and the limitless borrowing needs of government, business, and individuals.

Last but not least, Quigley asserts multiple times that the reins of power passed from "financial capitalism" to "monopoly capitalism" with the destruction of the gold standard.[34] (Once again, implying a loss of gold backing equaled a loss for those who wielded banking power.)

It would be easy enough to dismiss this supposed shift in power as a distinction without a difference because, at most, it amounted to a shift in methods of control rather than a shift in management. (The same Network that controlled financial capitalism paved the way for monopoly

---

33 *Tragedy and Hope,* page 257
34 Some references: *Tragedy and Hope,* pages 50, 62, 79, 338, and 502

capitalism, and the primary leader of the Network, Lord Milner himself, had written of his desire to abandon the gold standard as early as 1923.)[35] But there is a larger point to be made here.

If "monopoly capitalism" is *all powerful* because it can self-finance, manipulate the price of goods within its market, and use its inflated monopolistic profits to wield monetary influence, then there are no words to sufficiently describe the power of "financial capitalism."

- Not only can financial capitalists "self-finance," they can do so by simply creating money out of thin air and loaning it to others at interest. (What could possibly be more powerful than that?)
- Not only can financial capitalists manipulate the price of goods in a *particular* market, they can manipulate the price of goods in *any* market. (Real estate, food, energy, stocks, bonds, education…anything that has a price will be affected by those who manipulate the quantity and flow of money.)
- Not only do financial capitalists enjoy the influence of monopolistic profits, they enjoy the influence of having monopolized the creation of money itself. Stated another way: when a "monopoly capitalist" accumulates his first billion dollars, it's only because others have borrowed that billion dollars into existence from the Network's banking system.[36]

If Quigley truly understood the Network's banking system, he would have never fallen for the lie, undoubtedly perpetuated by the Network itself, that banking power peaked in the 1930s. The exact opposite is true. It wasn't

35 *The Anglo-American Establishment*, pages 122 and 123
36 For more information on how the money-creation process works, see MeetTheSystem. org, chapter 8

until the 1930s that international bankers began chipping away at the limitations of gold and inching the world ever closer to a purely debt-based standard.

As powerful as the Network's position was under the gold standard, it has increased immeasurably under their 100-percent debt-based standard. They can now create, destroy, and direct as much money as they see fit. They currently earn interest on every single dollar in existence, because every single dollar in existence has been *created and loaned* into the economy by them.

Accordingly, their debt-based system guarantees that nations will remain forever trapped in debt. (As a nation and its citizens attempt to reduce their debt to bankers, they simultaneously reduce their nation's money supply. Paying off *all* debt would reduce the money supply to zero...not only would this be impossible, but financial chaos and "emergency government borrowing" would be triggered long before any significant reduction in debt was achieved.) This is *not* a system that was designed with our best interests in mind.

In the next chapter, we'll cover the Network's banking system in more detail. We'll also cover the steps that we must take to free ourselves from their illegitimate monetary control.

CHAPTER 5
The Main Problem—The Main Solution

So far we've covered how the Network uses money to control governments, businesses, and trusted institutions. We've touched on how it developed ingenious ways to control other people's financial resources—their savings accounts, their insurance payments, and even their *income*. We've also gone over its greatest swindle of all: granting itself the legal authority to *create money* out of thin air.

With all of these monetary tools at its disposal, the Network has secretly and systematically consolidated its power over global policies that affect the lives of billions of human beings. Unelected, its members operate beyond the reach of voters. Unaccountable, they violate national and international laws with impunity. Obviously, if we intend to unseat them, we cannot continue playing by the rules of the system that *they* have created. We must be prepared to think and act in unapproved ways, and that begins with striking the root of their power…money.

In short, our adversary is using our own purchasing power against us. The money that we place in its institutions, the money we allow it to confiscate, and the money we allow it to *create*—these revenue streams provide the Network *trillions* of dollars each year to direct as it likes. Until we cut this funding, we are only wasting our time.

On the other side of the equation, these trillions of dollars represent the Network's Achilles' heel. Without access to this money, it cannot continue to purchase the people and resources necessary to defend its dominant position. (Their system is completely dependent upon the purchasing power that we provide.)

Knowing this, the answer to our dilemma seems very simple: reclaim our purchasing power and destroy their illegitimate system in the process. And truthfully, it really *is* that simple. But before getting into the obvious ways in which we can take back what is ours, there is one final twist in this story of monetary power. First, we must dig a little deeper into the story of money itself.

Few realize that money comes in many different forms. A basic list would include commodity money, receipt money, fractional money, fiat money, and debt money. (This isn't as complicated as it sounds; each form will be explained shortly.) Some of these forms of money are far easier to abuse than others, with the last one on the list (debt money) being the worst. Debt money is actually designed to enslave those who use it. No surprise then that debt money is what the Network has chosen to create and spread to all corners of the globe.

> Although slavery was abolished...many of the poor were reduced to peonage by contracting debts... binding themselves and their heirs to work for their creditors until the debt was paid. Such debt could never be paid in many cases, because the rate at which it was reduced was left to the creditor and could rarely be questioned by the illiterate debtor.[1]

This quote reveals that there is more than one way to reduce human beings to servitude. Though Quigley is

---

1 *Tragedy and Hope*, page 157

referencing a tactic that was used in mid-nineteenth century India, he perfectly captures the spirit of the financial system we live under today. It is a system that creates debt that "can never be paid," is "binding" on future generations, and is serviced by a global population of "illiterate" debtors.

Today, the term "illiterate debtor" has nothing to do with an individual's ability to read, write, or perform basic math. A person can possess all of these skills and still remain completely illiterate when it comes to understanding the Network's debt-based monetary system. Also, the indignities of "peonage" are no longer reserved exclusively for the poor. A person (or nation) can be poor or they can be rich; it makes little difference. Those who create and control the debt-money supply can manipulate the system and extract wealth from *everyone* who uses their currency. Not even those who are debt-free are safe. To the extent a person's income, savings, and assets are debt-money denominated, their purchasing power and accumulated wealth are at risk.

Since most people dislike being ripped off and exploited, it's reasonable to assume that the only reason the masses tolerate this debt-money system is because they do not understand how it works. That being the case, this chapter will attempt (in just a handful of pages) to end the financial illiteracy that the Network absolutely *depends on*. Consider this a super-abbreviated crash course on the topic, excerpted mainly from *Dishonest Money: Financing the Road to Ruin.*

What Is Money?

To accurately define what money is, we can't simply hold up a US dollar or a Russian ruble or a Mexican peso and say "This is money." We're better off to start by defining the overall purpose of money. What does money *do*?

In the simplest terms, money enables us to purchase products and services from other people. Using this basic description, we might go on to say **money *can be* anything that is widely accepted as *payment* for products and services.** Having defined money in this way, it will be easier to explain the different forms of money and why some are far more *honest* than others. But first, let's quickly touch on what existed before money—barter.

Barter

Prior to the creation of money, individuals used barter to trade with one another. This simply means that they would "purchase" what they wanted with products or services rather than paying for it with money. As an example, assume your neighbor grows corn, has one hundred extra pounds of it, and you would like some. If you grow tomatoes, it's possible that your neighbor will allow you to "buy" some of his corn using your tomatoes instead of money. Or, maybe he'll allow you to provide a service of some sort in exchange for his corn. (Perhaps you're good at building storage sheds, and he needs help building one.)

If the two of you are able to come to a barter agreement, then each of you will gain value from the exchange. (Your neighbor turns his surplus corn into something *he'd* rather have; you turn your surplus tomatoes or a couple days' work into something *you'd* rather have.) However, if your neighbor isn't interested in your tomatoes, and if he doesn't need a new storage shed, then both of you lose out. Both of you will have to find another trading partner.

Though limited, barter at least provided an *opportunity* for individuals (and society as a whole), to enjoy the benefits of trade. Rather than just having really good tomatoes and some nice storage sheds, you could also have some really good corn, really good wheat, clothes, furniture, or anything else that others had to offer. But again, you could only obtain these things if others wanted what *you* had to offer in exchange. This was the big limitation of barter, and it was overcome with the creation of commodity money.

Commodity Money

While trading with each other, people eventually realized that certain commodities were always in high demand. For instance, they discovered corn was so high in demand that it could consistently be traded for nearly anything. From that point forward, corn took on a value that exceeded its *consumption value*. In other words, even though your neighbor already had all the corn he needed, he would continue to grow (or acquire) more because he knew the corn would be accepted as payment for the products and services of others. The more corn he had, the more purchasing power he had. In this way, many different commodities (corn, wheat, cows, sheep, etc.) eventually evolved into reliable forms of commodity money. But just as barter had its limitations, so too did early forms of commodity money. These problems were eventually overcome when metal was discovered.

Unlike livestock, metal didn't need to be fed, watered, and cleaned up after. Unlike wheat and corn, you didn't have to worry about metal going bad, becoming contaminated with bugs, growing mold in storage, and so on. Also, metal was easily divisible. Assuming a milk cow was equal in value to one hundred pounds of iron, and the sale price of an item was twenty-five pounds of iron (or one-fourth of a milk cow), the individual buying with iron had a distinct advantage: he could easily produce the exact amount of money needed. For these reasons, metal eventually became the commodity money of choice, and though many different types of metal were used (iron, copper, and tin to name a few), gold and silver coins became the standard around the world.

Summary of Barter and Commodity Money

Both commodity money *and* barter share a couple of desirable attributes. The first attribute is transparency. If I want to trade my goat for some of your corn, I'll have to bring my goat and you'll have to bring some corn. The odds of either of us walking away with something else in our pocket, like a cricket, are pretty slim. Likewise, if I offer to buy something from you with a Gold Eagle (US gold coin), I must hand over a Gold Eagle. There is little chance that you will be duped into accepting a far less valuable Silver Eagle as payment for your item.

The second desirable attribute is the *intrinsic value* of the items traded. There are significant natural barriers that limit the production of commodities and, as such, their intrinsic value is transferred to anyone who acquires them. The person who acquires corn does not have to grow and harvest the corn himself; the person who earns a gold coin does not have to dig the gold out of the ground, fashion it into a coin, and convince others of its authenticity. Nobody can simply create gold, corn, or a goat with the flick of a pen. For this reason, these items will always possess the intrinsic value of the labor and the other costs that produced them.

These two attributes (transparency and intrinsic value) made it reasonably difficult to defraud people in trade because it isn't easy to convince somebody that you've paid them with a goat when, in fact, you've handed them a cricket. But just as barter led to the invention of commodity money, and commodity money eventually evolved into metal coins made from gold and silver, the inconveniences of gold and silver coins eventually led to the creation of a new form of money. And with it, the ability to easily defraud people (the ability to create money with "the flick of a pen") was born.

Receipt Money

Gold and silver coins were a much improved form of commodity money, but they still had some drawbacks. For instance, if you were even moderately wealthy, finding a place to safely store your coins was difficult. Also, if you wanted to make a large purchase or simply wanted to move a significant amount of money from one place to another, the weight of gold and silver coins made it challenging and nearly impossible to conceal. (Just sixteen hundred dollars in a silver-coin economy would have weighed approximately one hundred pounds!)[2] As before, these two problems were eventually solved. This time, the solution came from goldsmiths.

Goldsmiths already handled large stockpiles of gold and silver in their trade and had built very strong and well-guarded vaults to protect those stockpiles. This made solving the first problem (safe storage of gold and silver coins) a no-brainer. Goldsmiths began renting unused space in their vaults to citizens who wanted to keep their coins safe until they were needed. The goldsmith was happy to collect a fee from each depositor, and the depositors were happy to know that their money was in good hands. Interestingly enough, the safe-storage solution ended up solving the weight problem of using coins in trade as well.

When a citizen came in to deposit their coins for storage, the goldsmith would hand the depositor a paper receipt as

---

2 The term *dollar* used to have a very specific meaning. For a dollar to be a dollar, it had to be a coin that contained nearly one ounce of fine silver (http://en.wikipedia.org/wiki/Spanish_dollar#United_States). The Network has nearly destroyed that definition. Today, we all believe we have "dollars," when, in truth, all we've got is pieces of paper with the word "dollar" printed on them.

proof of their deposit. So, if a customer deposited $1,000 in gold coins, they were given a receipt (or receipts) valued at $1,000 worth of gold. These receipts were marked "payable on demand," meaning anyone, at any time, could come in and exchange the receipts for gold. Because the receipts were literally as "good as gold," citizens began accepting them as payment for products and services. From that point forward, the receipts became a new form of money: receipt money. Though the receipts were only made of paper, each one was 100 percent backed by gold (or sometimes silver) and, therefore, each receipt was a legitimate form of paper money.

However, as time passed it became increasingly rare for individuals to cash in their receipts and withdraw coins from the goldsmith's vault. Assuming their coins were safe and always available, depositors had no reason to remove them. (They'd just have to find another safe place to store them if they did.) Besides, it was much easier to use the receipt money in commerce. Nearly all citizens preferred to carry a pocket full of the goldsmith's receipts to a pocket full of heavy coins.

Now, put yourself in the goldsmith's shoes. The receipts that *you create* are trusted by all. They're literally considered as "good as gold" and are accepted as payment for products and services, just the same as if a person paid with a gold or silver coin. Although you do not possess the power to create gold and silver coins "with the flick of a pen," you *do* possess the power to create receipts that are every bit as valuable in trade. What do you do?

Fractional Money

It wasn't long before goldsmiths realized that they could simply print up additional receipts for their own benefit. This, of course, was an act of pure fraud. Each ounce of depositors' gold held in the goldsmith's vault had a corresponding receipt that was issued to the gold's rightful owner. Issuing additional receipts constituted a theft of purchasing power, and worse, it set into motion the inevitable loss of the depositor's coins.

To illustrate, say a man walks into the goldsmith's shop, deposits $1,000 worth of gold, and receives $1,000 worth of receipts in exchange. No problem there. An hour later, another man comes into the goldsmith's shop, but he doesn't want to make a deposit; he wants to *borrow* $1,000. The goldsmith agrees to the loan and issues the borrower $1,000 worth of *new* receipts, which are created on the spot. There is now $2,000 worth of receipts, but only $1,000 worth of gold in the vault.

Now imagine that the borrower takes his newly created $1,000 worth of receipts to a local store and spends them. And say the store owner decides he'd rather have the actual gold coins instead of the paper. So, he takes the receipts to the goldsmith, cashes them in for coins, and goes on his way. Everyone is happy to this point. But what happens if an hour later the man who made the original $1,000 gold-coin deposit shows up to withdraw his coins? Too bad for him. His gold walked out the door an hour earlier when the *loaned* receipts (created without a corresponding deposit) were cashed in.

This is a highly simplified example, but it illustrates the problem that emerged with the creation of paper-receipt money: it opened the door to fraud. What began as a legitimate form of paper money, backed 100 percent by coins held in reserve, eventually turned into *fractional money*. And as the goldsmith printed more and more receipts, the *fraction* of coins backing those receipts became less and less.

Before long, citizens were unknowingly accepting receipts backed by only half of the receipt's printed value, a quarter of its printed value, a tenth of its printed value.

When people finally figured out what was going on, they rushed to exchange their receipts for the coins that rightfully belonged to them. Of course, only the first few in line were able to withdraw their gold and silver. All the rest were left holding worthless paper.

Fiat Money

In the previous example, people accepted paper receipts in exchange for their products and services for one reason: they thought that they could cash in their receipts for gold or silver coins whenever they wanted. None of them knew that they were essentially selling their goods for inadequately backed pieces of paper. If they had known the receipts were fraudulent, they wouldn't have accepted them; they would have demanded actual coins instead. Clearly, they were ripped off.

Again, in an economy that uses *only* commodity money (as opposed to paper money), it is very difficult to rip people off because the actual commodity must be surrendered at the time of purchase. The trade is transparent. But in the aforementioned receipt-money economy, only the *assumption* of transparency exists. Yes, the receipt *might* actually be legitimate; it might represent an underlying commodity that physically exists and does not belong to anyone else. However, it might also be illegitimate. You might sell an ounce of gold for a more-convenient receipt that's marked "one ounce of gold," only to find out later that your receipt can't be redeemed for anything. If this happens, it's very clear who won and who lost in the exchange. (What thief wouldn't want to trade worthless receipts for as many ounces of gold as he could get? Printing paper receipts is very easy...Printing gold is impossible.)

This reminds us of what money is *supposed* to be: something that enables us to purchase the products and services of others. The *only* reason we are willing to work for money is because we believe the money we earn will serve this purpose. Nobody interested in earning money would exchange their time and effort for pieces of paper that they *knew* to be worthless. Therefore if somebody wants to use paper money to steal from others, the most obvious way is to mislead them into believing that the money has value. However, *fiat money* provides another way to steal: good old-fashioned government force.

Encarta defines fiat money as: "paper money that a government declares to be legal tender although it is not based on or convertible into coins."

Another way to put that would be: fiat money is paper money, backed by nothing, and the government forces people to accept it via legal tender laws. It's basically the goldsmith's counterfeit receipts on steroids. Whereas the goldsmith had to conceal the fact that he was fraudulently printing money to enrich and empower himself, fiat money enables a group like the Network to openly print money and force it down people's throats. They simply use their law-making ability to *legalize* the scam.

Whether by fraud or by fiat, the power to print money is the power to steal whatever money can buy. Fiat money is more egregious because, unlike fraud, it is backed by force and can be used to openly confiscate purchasing power on an enormous scale. (There is no doubt that the Network advanced its position significantly when it moved the United States from a gold- and silver-backed money supply to a purely fiat model.) But believe it or not, there is actually something worse than fiat paper money. And this brings us to the final form of money we'll be discussing in this "crash course," the form of money we use today—debt money.

Debt Money

Take the inherently fraudulent characteristics of the goldsmith's fractional money system, add in the greater fraud and *force* of pure fiat, top it off with a mechanism designed to generate inescapable debt, and presto: you've got the most sophisticated monetary-enslavement system ever devised by man. And, wouldn't you know, you also have all the components that make up our current monetary system.

Unlike a normal fiat money system (where the ruling class simply creates its own worthless paper money, spends it into the economy, and demands that everyone accept it), our ruling class has devised something much more powerful. Rather than *spend* money into our economy, they *loan* money into our economy. This enables the Network to steal purchasing power from us twice: once when they create new money, and again as they collect interest on the *entire* money supply.

Worst of all, by creating money and putting it into circulation *only* when a loan is made, and then *destroying* that same money (removing it from circulation) when the loan is repaid, the Network has designed the perfect debt trap. Any meaningful attempt to escape this debt trap, by paying down debt, will trigger an automatic "correction mechanism" that *guarantees* failure. The chain of events is perfectly predictable: as the nation repays its banking debts (and refuses to take out new loans), the economy's debt-based money supply will shrink. This will cause disruptions in the economy; initially the disruptions will be minor, but they will inevitably become intolerable if new money isn't injected via new loans. (Imagine the consequences of a 10 percent reduction in the nation's money supply...now imagine a 40 percent reduction, a 60 percent reduction, or an 80 percent reduction.)

Theoretically, if new loans are not issued to reverse the automatic "correction mechanism" that the Network has built into the system, and if all available funds continue to be applied toward extinguishing Network-created debt, then the debt-based money supply must eventually fall to *zero*.

Robert Hemphill was the credit manager of the Federal Reserve Bank in Atlanta. In the foreword to a book by Irving Fisher, entitled *100% Money*, Hemphill said this:

> If all the bank loans were paid, no one could have a bank deposit, and there would not be a dollar of coin or currency in circulation. This is a staggering thought. We are completely dependent on the commercial banks. Someone has to borrow every dollar we have…If the banks create ample synthetic money we are prosperous; if not, we starve. We are absolutely without a permanent money system. When one gets a complete grasp of the picture, the tragic absurdity of our hopeless situation is almost incredible—but there it is.[3]

Needless to say, the economic and political power that flows from this system is nothing short of obscene. Therefore, it's easy to understand why the Network built this system like a prison. Playing by their rules, we cannot escape; we can *never* repay the debt that is owed. And just like the debt slaves of nineteenth-century India, this inescapable debt is binding on our children, and our children's children, and so on…forever.

Of all the Network's monetary powers, *this* particular power is the most destructive. In nation after nation, politicians who are happy to bury their citizens in debt are

---

3 *The Creature From Jekyll Island*, page 188

supported by the Network and placed into positions of power. Some of the politicians are well intentioned; others are not. In the end it really doesn't matter. As politically motivated spending programs (from warfare to welfare) spiral out of control, it isn't long before massive monthly loans are needed just to cover the day-to-day operating costs of government. The noose is then tightened further with a never-ending slate of *new* spending programs that are added year after year, decade after decade. Out of the crushing debt that ensues, and the subsequent need for an endless supply of new loans to keep the bankrupt system afloat, the Network secures its dominant position over everything and everyone that depends on its money.

In the meantime, the illiterate debtors of the world slave away with no idea that the money they "owe" was created out of thin air; it was never *earned* by the lender. They have no idea that the system itself was designed to create an ever-expanding black hole of debt, a system of financial servitude that is literally inescapable.

> Those conspiring to bring us a "world government" ruled by an "intellectual elite and world bankers" are not playing games. They've worked hard to perfect and implement their strategy of economic conquest. They've proven their ability to seize control of nations large and small (even far-flung empires). They certainly haven't come all this way for nothing.[4]

How Many Are Willing to Fight?

There isn't enough room here to cover how inflation, deflation, booms, busts, and bailouts all provide additional

---

4 *Dishonest Money*, page 65

ways for the Network to transfer wealth and power into its own hands. For now, it's enough to reiterate the opening claim of this chapter: money is the root of the Network's power. For them to dominate "all the habitable portions of the world,"[5] they absolutely *must* maintain their ability to confiscate, create, and control the money that we earn. And since they will never surrender these monetary weapons willingly, our only choice is to forcibly disarm them.

> "The whole history of the progress of human liberty shows that all concessions yet made...have been born of earnest struggle...This struggle may be a moral one; or it may be a physical one; or it may be both moral and physical; but it must be a struggle. Power concedes nothing without a demand. It never did and it never will. Find out just what a people will submit to, and you have found out the exact amount of injustice and wrong which will be imposed upon them; and these will continue till they are resisted with either words or blows, or with both. The limits of tyrants are prescribed by the endurance of those whom they oppress."—Frederick Douglass[6]

The Network is literally composed of criminals who hide behind the "legitimacy" of government to *force* their will on us all. Their power over our debt-money system, their power to tax our incomes and wage war on national sovereignty, their relentless expansion of the government that *they* control—all of this power has been taken by force and fraud. They're not going to turn the "government power" they have created against themselves (any more than an armed robber would turn his own gun against himself in defense

---

5 *Tragedy and Hope*, page 131
6 http://en.wikiquote.org/wiki/Frederick_Douglass

of his victims). No, to reclaim what is rightfully ours, we are going to have to fight...and this leads to one final problem.

Time and time again, history has shown that the predator class will do whatever is necessary to gain and keep the reins of power. In fact, those who subscribe to the concept of "survival of the fittest" would almost certainly argue in the Network's defense. Its members have studied rulers of the past, improved upon ancient techniques of propaganda and mass manipulation, and have thus *earned* their right to rule. Following this logic, the same survival-of-the-fittest crowd would argue that the masses belong exactly where they are: *beneath* the ruling class. Without the willful ignorance, indifference, and timidity of the subjugated, our rulers simply could not exist. It is a symbiotic relationship, one of parasite and host. Society's refusal to even acknowledge (let alone remove) the bulging tick that's stuck to its forehead is akin to consent. This being the case, why shouldn't the Network continue gorging itself?

Does this position blame the victims? Perhaps...but sometimes the victims deserve a little blame.

The typical voter has chosen to accept a fairly obvious lie: that the government is an instrument of *the people*, that it is subject to the *will of the governed*, and nobody (inside or outside of government) is above the law. To these voters, the idea of a highly organized shadow government, operating at the direct expense of the governed, is laughed off without investigation. They might passionately believe that Republicans are corrupt and only the Democrats can save them, or that Democrats are corrupt and only Republicans can save them, but they have yet to recognize the deeper truth: neither Republicans nor Democrats are ever going to save them. Both sides are funded and maintained by the same ruling class to create the *illusion* of choice.

To really drive this point home, let's revisit a few earlier quotes. First from Quigley:

It is increasingly clear that, in the twentieth century, the expert **will replace...the democratic voter in control of the political system**...Hopefully, the elements of choice and freedom may survive for the ordinary individual in that he may be free to make a choice between two opposing political groups (even if these groups have little policy choice within the parameters of policy established by the experts)...**in general, his freedom and choice will be controlled within very narrow alternatives.**[7]

And again, our "expert" on scientific manipulation, Bertrand Russell, takes the concept of hidden power a step further: the experts will not only target the electorate for manipulation, they will target the *elected* as well:

The government, being an oligarchy...**may invent ingenious ways of concealing its own power**, leaving the forms of democracy intact, and allowing the plutocrats or politicians to imagine that they are cleverly controlling these forms...whatever the outward forms may be, **all real power will come to be concentrated in the hands of those who understand the art of scientific manipulation.**[8]

Finally, from the father of propaganda himself, Edward Bernays:

The conscious manipulation of the masses is an important element in democratic society. Those who manipulate this unseen mechanism of society constitute an invisible government which is **the true ruling power of our country.**

7 *Tragedy and Hope,* page 866
8 *The Scientific Outlook,* page 175

To summarize the substance of this problem: the majority of the population does not understand how they're being manipulated, nor do they see a bulging tick stuck to society's forehead. They see only the image of *government* that the "true ruling power" wants them to see. And if they continue turning exclusively to the same ruling power for all of their information, their perception will never change. That's why, if we want as many fighters as possible, we're going to have to speak up. We're going to have to counter the "conscious manipulation of the masses."

Solutions—Where to Begin

This short section of the book will be the easiest to write. That's because there isn't anything particularly complicated about how to free ourselves from financial and political servitude.[9] In a nutshell, it boils down to this: the Network's empire is built entirely on stolen financial power and manufactured consent. **Our objective is to undermine both of these, one mind and one dollar at a time, until the Network can no longer defend itself in any meaningful way**. That's it.

Now, the question becomes: What are the steps we should take to achieve this objective? Although there are many options, implementation of the following will absolutely devastate the Network's power.

1. Raise Awareness: Expose Their Illegitimacy

This is not only the easiest step; it is arguably the most important. Reach out to new people regularly and share information that exposes what the Network is and how it operates. When you encounter individuals who either refuse to look at the facts, or who minimize the

---

9 I wish I could say the same about *preventing the recurrence* of the exact same problem under a new group of ruling elite, but that's another story for a later time.

significance of what's presented, do not take it personally. If they attack you, do not take it personally. In most cases, they are simply defending their world view...It has nothing to do with *you*. Simply move on and know that *every single person* that is exposed to this information, even those who initially resist, *could* become an ally down the road. The same cannot be said of those who are never exposed to the truth.

2. Competing Currencies: Stop Using the Network's Money

"End the Fed!" is the rallying cry of millions who have learned how the Network's "Federal Reserve System" was created and how it operates. This privately owned and controlled money machine has been rightfully identified as the heart of the enemy's power. To truly disarm the Network, we first must *end* its ability to create and control our money supply. This can be done, but it won't be easy.

The good news is that anti-Fed sentiment is growing every day. The bad news is that the Network is already manipulating this sentiment, steering well-intentioned critics toward *nationalizing* the Fed. But nationalizing the Fed will not end its ability to create and control our money supply. In fact, this is the same tactic the Network used with the Central Bank of England when demands to end its private ownership reached a fevered pitch. Though nationalization *did* end outright private ownership of the bank, it did little to affect the Network's *control*.[10]

---

10 Even Quigley noted, upon the nationalization of the Bank of England, that the same powers that dominated the bank prior to nationalization "strangely enough, still have retained some of this, despite the nationalization of the Bank by the Labour government in 1946." *Tragedy and Hope*, page 500

For an idea of how *nationalization* of the Fed would unfold in the United States, flash back to how the Federal Reserve System was created in the first place (in response to public demands for financial reform, covered in chapter 4). The *visible* US government will spring into action to "protect the people" from out-of-control bankers, and it will accomplish the exact opposite in the process.[11]

Our best move against the Network's control of our money supply is to begin developing and using competing currencies—money that literally *competes* with the Network's fraudulent debt money that circulates in the economy. This move accomplishes two important functions: (1) it cuts the Network out of the equation when we buy and sell from one another, and (2) it protects us in the event of a Network-initiated run on the dollar.[12]

Gold and silver are the two most obvious forms of money that we could begin using, and some states, aware of the dangers of the current monetary system, have begun pushing legislation that will make gold and silver legal tender again. But gold and silver aren't the only options. Digital currencies like Bitcoin, Litecoin, and even Dogecoin[13] are gaining traction among millions of citizens around the world, without any sanction from government whatsoever.[14] In addition to these digital currencies, there is also

---

11 For additional arguments against nationalizing the Federal Reserve System, there is a short article available here: JoePlummer.com/let-government-print-the-money.html
12 The Network wants to eventually replace the dollar with a one-world currency. To force the United States, and other nations who depend on the dollar, into the new currency, it will likely cause a dollar panic and then put the new currency forward as a "temporary/emergency solution to get trade moving again." The greater the financial and social chaos, the less likely any nation will have the power to resist. However, if there are already other viable currencies in place that can facilitate trade without major disruptions to the economy, there will be no need for the citizens of the world to accept an expanded debt-denominated, slave-money system.
13 Dogecoin, though it actually began as a joke, established a strong community of users by March 2014.
14 For a short article and video on Bitcoin, visit: http://joeplummer.com/bitcoin-vs-federal-reserve-notes.html

the option of competing private currencies, community currencies, time-based currencies, and so on.

The key point is to remember why the Network created central banks in the first place: to control "the political system of each country and the economy of the world as a whole."[15] The sooner we develop effective ways to trade outside of their system, the sooner their system will become irrelevant and we can ignore it into oblivion.

3. Attack the Income Tax

In chapter 4, we went over how the Network, approximately one hundred years ago, began stealing massive amounts of money for its global-domination project. It called the theft "income tax" and has glorified the annual expropriation as a citizen's "moral duty" ever since.

It's beyond the scope of this text to delve into how the Network, acting through its *tax-exempt* foundations, has used education to build public support for this previously illegal confiscation of wages.[16] Suffice to say, using government as its instrument, the Network can now funnel trillions of dollars each year into furthering its own interests. From multitrillion-dollar banker bailouts, to the approximately one hundred million dollars *per hour* gushing into the military industrial complex,[17] the Network can

---

15 *Tragedy and Hope*, page 324
16 The topic of how the Network has used education to "pull the strings of the public mind" is enormous and well worth looking into. If you want a short introduction, I recommend Ed Griffin's interview of Norman Dodd. The transcript is available here: http://www.realityzone.com/hiddenagenda2.html
17 This is a term made popular by President Eisenhower in his farewell address. He stated, in part: "In the councils of government, we must guard against the acquisition of unwarranted influence...by the military-industrial complex. The potential for the disastrous rise of misplaced power exists and will persist...We should take nothing for granted. Only an alert and knowledgeable citizenry can compel the proper meshing of the huge industrial and military machinery of defense with our peaceful methods and goals, so that security and liberty may prosper together." http://en.wikipedia.org/wiki/Eisenhower's_farewell_address

legally accomplish things with "government taxation" and "government policy" that it could never accomplish privately.

Of course, *private power* disguised as government power is hardly a new phenomenon, and those who founded the United States federal government did everything they could to protect us from this problem. They knew that the more powerful the government became, the sooner it would be corrupted for private use. That is why our Constitution was written to *limit* government power. Our Bill of Rights was written to *limit* government power. The Founders' opposition to standing armies, their stance against fiat paper money, their aversion to taxation—all of these served to *limit* government power and, by extension, the inevitable private abuse of that power. Unfortunately, the Network has relentlessly undermined or outright destroyed *all* of the aforementioned limits, one by one, since 1913.

This perfectly illustrates *why* we must sever, or severely disrupt, their so-called "income-tax" funding mechanism. Forget the fact that it was foisted on the nation via fraud and manipulation. Forget the fact that the revenue is being used to destroy (rather than protect) the substance of our Constitution and Bill of Rights. Instead, view the argument against a compulsory income tax purely from the angle of a *power* relationship. View it the way the Network views it: if the citizenry can *force* the "government" to obey its wishes (by cutting off access to money), then the citizens have the final say on whether or not a policy decision will survive. However, if men with power can simply confiscate whatever amount of money they want (via taxes or via the printing press), then the citizens have lost their most effective nonviolent method of control. Yes, they can still express massive disapproval, as they did in the case of the most recent banker bailouts, but this means nothing. As long as the complaints are submitted with *payment in full,* and all of the outrage over the government's refusal to listen falls on easily replaceable representatives, the Network's power remains undisturbed.

Ultimately, each individual must decide how to attack the income-tax issue. I myself decided to cut my income drastically, eventually reducing the amount of money I "owed" to zero.[18] This is probably too radical for most people, and there are certainly other options. Some find legal ways to reduce their income taxes; others engage in not-so-legal ways. Some continue "paying with complaint" (which is at least better than paying *without* complaint), while others flatly refuse to pay at all. Last but not least, competing currencies also provide an option because they enable citizens to conduct trade outside of the Network's financial system. Whether it's with gold and silver coins, or semianonymous digital currencies like Bitcoin, Litecoin, or Dogecoin, the inability of the Network to easily track these transactions makes it difficult for its members to calculate what is "owed."[19] It's then up to the citizens to decide what duty they have to disclose their private financial affairs to men who are openly trying to enslave them.

It goes without saying that the founding fathers would have considered the income tax an unconstitutional abomination. It goes without saying that the Network used its illegitimate influence to foist this tax on the American people.

---

18 By 2003, I was painfully aware of the illegitimate nature of our federal government. Due to the amount of money I was making at the time (roughly $500,000 per year), my so-called income taxes, even after deductions, were running in excess of $100,000 annually. There is no way I can express how *compromised* I felt each time I wrote one of those checks, knowing full well that I was empowering individuals who were actively engaged in the destruction of my country. So, I resolved to sell my business and do everything I could to expose their crimes, living mostly off of savings and revenue from whatever assets I could sell. Ten years later, I've finally run out of savings and assets, but I don't regret my decision. It feels good to know, at the very least, I saved myself the angst of handing over another $1 million or more in "taxes" to a gang of liars, thieves, and tyrants. Regretfully, now that I must start earning money again, I will have to face this conflict again.
19 Of course, "the government" is already working to create a regulatory environment that will destroy this advantage.

It should have never existed. It ought to be repealed and replaced with, preferably, nothing. (The Federal government carried out its *intended* role in our society, without an income tax, for more than a century. It can do so again.)

4. Nullification: Refuse to Comply, Refuse to Convict

Practically forgotten, the extremely powerful weapon of *nullification* has recently been dusted off and is being put to good use. The concept behind nullification is very simple: *the people* determine what the government has the power to do, not the other way around. When policy makers in Washington grant themselves "legal authority" to do things that violate the legal restrictions on their power, the people have the right and the *duty* to restrain them.

> Two dozen American states nullified the REAL ID Act of 2005. More than a dozen states have successfully defied the federal government over medical marijuana. Nullification initiatives of all kinds, involving the recent health care legislation, cap and trade, and the Second Amendment are popping up everywhere.
>
> The indispensable source for developments connected to nullification [can be found at] TenthAmendmentCenter.com. Its Legislative Tracking page covers a variety of nullification initiatives and tracks their progress in state legislatures across the country.[20]

---

20 For a quick introduction to nullification, visit: http://www.libertyclassroom.com/nullification/

State nullification, even the *threat* of state nullification, is a tool that has been used effectively for hundreds of years in this country. From the Alien and Sedition Acts of 1798 to the unconstitutional searches and seizures of 1807–1809, from resistance to conscription in 1812 to the northern states' obstruction of the fugitive-slave laws, nullification has provided a nonviolent way for citizens to push back against federal overreach.[21] But state nullification isn't our only option. Another form is *jury* nullification, and it has the potential to be even more powerful.

> Jury nullification occurs when a jury concludes that a defendant is technically guilty, but fails to convict the defendant on the grounds that the law in question is unjust. While jury nullification is legal, judges frequently do not inform juries of this power...[22]
>
> In the United States, jury nullification first appeared in the pre-Civil War era when juries sometimes refused to convict for violations of the Fugitive Slave Act. Later, during Prohibition, juries often nullified alcohol control laws, possibly as often as 60% of the time. This resistance may have contributed to the adoption of the Twenty-first amendment repealing Prohibition...[23]

To demonstrate the enormity of this *direct* power we were given over our government, imagine the following hypothetical scenario: I am a juror, and you have been dragged into court for refusing to pay your taxes to the Network's collection instrument (the IRS.) Unrepentant, you stand and state the following: "I will no longer voluntarily

---

21 http://www.libertyclassroom.com/objections/
22 http://www.huffingtonpost.com/2012/09/17/doug-darrell-marijuana-jury-nullification_n_1890824.html
23 http://en.wikipedia.org/wiki/Jury_nullification

fund an institution that violates the law with impunity and engages in morally reprehensible behavior. I will no longer be complicit in crime. I would rather be punished for obeying my conscience than be rewarded for ignoring it."

It's very unlikely that your defense attorney would support this approach, but remember that this is just a hypothetical scenario to demonstrate the power we *still possess* as citizens. If I'm a juror in this case, you better believe that I am going to argue for nullification. If that fails, I am going to ensure a hung jury. There will be no conviction this time around. Now, multiply that same scenario a couple dozen times, then a couple hundred times, and then a couple thousand times...the power over our incomes, *stolen* by the Network in 1913, will be rightfully returned to the people. (Laws that cannot be successfully prosecuted cannot survive. Nullification is our final nonviolent check on the abuse of government power.)

5. Disruptive Technologies

Over the past 100 years, the Network has worked very hard to monopolize our money, media, medicine, manufacturing, education, energy, agriculture, and government. But all of this top-down centralized power is currently under attack. It's being destroyed; not by armies, but by innovation.

As of now, the most obvious and widespread example of this monopoly-destroying power is the internet. Although the Network can still use its legacy-media empire to spread lies, the internet has dramatically cut the lifecycle of those lies. Also, thanks to the internet, the Network has lost its ability to stop whistleblowers, hackers, and ordinary citizens from exposing its crimes. (Before, it could simply refuse to distribute the evidence against it. Today, we can distribute the evidence ourselves; we can reach around the world instantly, at nearly zero cost.) In all of human history, rulers have never faced a threat of this magnitude, and it's only just beginning.

We are now entering an era of technological development that many believe will lead to "exponential disruption." All of the aforementioned choke points of control (from energy to education, medicine to manufacturing, agriculture to government) will change dramatically in the next 20 – 30 years. The most beneficial characteristic of these technology-driven changes is that they, like the internet, will decentralize and redistribute power. They will weaken, and then replace, the immoral and inadequate centralized systems that our rulers have created.

Simply stated, to disrupt the elite, we must continue decentralizing everything they have monopolized. We must build the competing / parallel systems that will eventually render their current systems irrelevant. And here is where the issue of "raising awareness" really shows its importance. For every 1 million people that "wake up," there will be a very small number who fully apply their talents (in their areas of expertise) toward creating solutions. As more join the fight, more solutions will emerge. Equally important are the millions who are "awake" but aren't actively developing solutions. Why? Because they will provide the vital base of early adopters; they will be the ones who support the emerging alternatives.

By the time 10 to 15 percent of the adult population begins to support and apply the tactics outlined in this chapter, the Network's continued illegitimate control will become unmanageable. But this army of informed and engaged citizens isn't going to magically appear. We have to make it happen. And as we're making it happen, those who currently hold power will attack our efforts with every lie and dirty trick in the book; but that doesn't matter. If we intend to take back what "false and designing men"[24] have stolen, we must be prepared to *demand* it. If we hope to achieve our ends via nonviolent means, the time to act is **now**...and if a violent confrontation proves unavoidable, we can rest assured that the *nonviolent* work we have done will provide the foundation for our success.

To clarify the importance of resistance, I will cover the incredible lawlessness and immorality of those we're up against in the final chapters. Rather than focus on how they *might* abuse their power, I'll focus on how they already have.

---

24 This is a reference to a famous quote by Samuel Adams. It reads, in part: "The liberties of our Country, the freedom of our civil constitution are worth defending at all hazards: And it is our duty to defend them against all attacks...It will bring an everlasting mark of infamy on the present generation, enlightened as it is, if we should suffer them to be wrested from us by violence without a struggle; or be cheated out of them by the artifices of false and designing men. Of the latter we are in most danger at present..." http://en.wikiquote.org/wiki/Samuel_Adams

CHAPTER 6

Rulers Represent Themselves

"Liberty cannot be preserved without a general knowledge among the people [of] that most dreaded and envied kind of knowledge, I mean of the characters and conduct of their rulers."

—John Adams[1]

In the Declaration of Independence, we find the primary argument for establishing government power: to secure the rights of the people. Without some type of protection mechanism in place, criminals will prey on the population without fear of consequences. They will do as they please to those who are too weak to resist them.

In the exact same document, we find the primary argument for *limiting* or *revoking* government power: to secure the rights of the people. Without some type of protection mechanism in place, criminals will gain control of government and use its power to prey on the population. They will do as they please to those who are too weak to resist them. (They will never use the power of government to prosecute and punish themselves.)

---

1 This quote carries a heavy dose of irony. Can there be true "liberty" if elected officials see themselves as "rulers"? And if John Adams *truly* believed in the concept of liberty, would he have ever signed the Alien and Sedition Acts into law?

The first argument (government can protect us from crime) is still alive and well. In fact, it's drilled relentlessly into every citizen's head from a very early age. However, the second argument (government can actually *subject us* to crime) has practically disappeared from politically correct conversation. This, despite the fact that the *threat* posed by criminals in government far exceeds any threat posed by common criminals. If there is any doubt, consider the following:

Common criminals do not have access to the media, the trust of the masses, or the air of legitimacy given to those who secure a position of *authority*. They cannot legally seize our money, destroy the purchasing power of our currency, or control the police and military. Common criminals cannot *legislate away* our rights, or reduce our children to debt slaves. They cannot obstruct an inquiry into their crimes from *inside* the system. (They cannot seal documents, confiscate and "lose" evidence, or appoint their own investigators.) Common criminals cannot write laws and *selectively* enforce them. They cannot disarm millions of their would-be victims, round them up and put them in cages, or worse. They cannot take nations to war, profiting financially and politically from the carnage...

Suffice to say, *this* is why those who created the US government spoke constantly about limiting its power via the Constitution and Bill of Rights. As Thomas Jefferson wrote in the *Kentucky Resolutions of 1798*, too much confidence in our elected leaders' good intentions is the "parent of despotism everywhere." It would be a "dangerous delusion," he warned, for us to trust those who currently hold power simply because they are "men of our choice."

> "In questions of power...let no more be heard of confidence in man, but bind him down from mis-

chief by the chains of the Constitution."—Thomas Jefferson, Kentucky Resolutions

Members of the Network have spent the past one hundred years doing everything in their power to nurture the "dangerous delusion" that Jefferson warned us about. Before they can have their way with the world, our rulers must break the "chains of the Constitution" that bind them down. They don't want to exercise *limited* government power; they want to exercise the opposite.

A War on Freedom

"Of all the enemies to public liberty war is, perhaps, the most to be dreaded...War is the parent of armies; from these proceed debts and taxes...and armies, and debts, and taxes are the known instruments for bringing the many under the domination of the few...No nation could preserve its freedom in the midst of continual warfare."—James Madison[2]

In chapter 1, we briefly covered the 1950s-era investigations into large, tax-exempt foundations. Many were shocked when it was discovered that the *capitalist* foundations were using their money to support *Communism*. At first glance, this seems ridiculous. Why would the wealthiest men in the world want to "orient American far eastern policies toward Communist objectives?"[3] This seemingly suicidal policy begins to make more sense when you learn how the Network actually operates. It's important to remember that war, and the *threat* of war, has enabled them (more than

---

2 http://en.wikiquote.org/wiki/James_Madison
3 Taken from the final report of the Senate Internal Security Subcommittee, http://en.wikipedia.org/wiki/Institute_of_Pacific_Relations

anything else) to inch ever closer to their goal of destroying national sovereignty.

Norman Dodd was the lead researcher for one of the aforementioned investigations[4] and, as such, he was chosen to appoint the committee's staff. By the 1950s, propaganda touting the humanitarian "benevolence" of the tax-exempt foundations was widely accepted and many people, including one of Dodd's researchers, Katherine Casey, felt that the foundations were beyond reproach. As Dodd put it, Casey was "unsympathetic to the purpose of the investigation. Her attitude...was: 'What could possibly be wrong with foundations? They do so much good.'"[5] But Casey's trust was soon shattered as she dug into what was, at the time, decades-old records of the Network-connected Carnegie Foundation. Dodd explains:

> I blocked out certain periods of time [for Casey] to concentrate on, and off she went to New York. She came back at the end of two weeks with the following on Dictaphone tapes:
>
> "We are now at the year 1908...In that year, the trustees...raised a specific question, which they discussed throughout the balance of the year in a very learned fashion. The question is: **'Is there any means known more effective than war, assuming you wish to alter the life of an entire people?'** And they conclude that no more effective means than war to that end is known to humanity. So then, in 1909, they raised the second question and discussed it, namely: **'How do we involve the United States in a war?'**...Then, finally, they answered that question as follows: **'We must control the State Department.'** That very naturally raises

---

4 http://en.wikipedia.org/wiki/The_Reece_Committee
5 Source: Ed Griffin's interview with Norman Dodd: http://www.realityzone.com/hiddenagenda2.html

the question of how do we do that? And they answer it by saying: **'We must take over and control the diplomatic machinery of this country.'** And, finally, they resolve to aim at that as an objective."

Keep in mind, the plans that Casey is reporting on were originally written just a few years *before* the Network managed to gain control of the "diplomatic machinery" of the country (using Woodrow Wilson and Mandell House). That control was later expanded via the Network-led group of "experts" known as *The Inquiry*. The Inquiry, in turn, evolved into what is now known as the Council on Foreign Relations. Within twenty years of its founding, the CFR's enormous power within the State Department was undeniable. (Look no further than the 1939 *War and Peace Studies* for an excellent example.[6]) Casey's report continues:

> "Then time passes, and we are eventually in a war, which would be World War I. At that time they record on their minutes a shocking report in which they dispatched to President Wilson a telegram, cautioning him to see that the war does not end too quickly. Finally, of course, the war is over. At that time their interest shifts over to preventing what they call a reversion of life in the United States to what it was prior to 1914 when World War I broke out. At that point they came to the conclusion that, to prevent a reversion, *'we must control education in the United States.'*...They realize that that's a pretty big task...

---

6 Today, there is a good deal of information available on the CFR-directed War and Peace Studies. However, the project was initially top secret, unknown to all but a handful of CFR members. In *Seeds of Destruction*, page 102, William Engdahl notes: "the War and Peace Studies Group of the New York Council on Foreign Relations, effectively took over all significant post-war planning for the US State Department. After 1942, most of its members were quietly put directly on the State Department payroll."

They then decide that the key to success…lay in the alteration of the teaching of American history."[7]

According to Norman Dodd, Casey was so devastated by the information she uncovered during the Reece Committee investigation that she never recovered.

As far as its impact on Katherine Casey was concerned…she never was able to return to her law practice. Ultimately, she lost her mind as a result of it. It was a terrible shock. It's a very rough experience to encounter proof of these kinds.[8]

That final sentence is profound. It actually *is* a very "rough experience to encounter proof" that you've been intentionally misled. It is *painful* to learn that intelligent, manipulative, and arrogant liars have secured your well-meaning trust, only then to play you as a fool. *Nobody* wants to face that feeling and, as it relates to "our" powerful institutions, that feeling gets worse before it gets better. After discovering the initial betrayal, you come to realize that your trust has been betrayed at every turn. You realize that the entire system has been *designed* to deceive and trap you (along with the rest of the unsuspecting public) in a fabricated reality, in an illusion.

Perhaps worst of all, after some study and serious thought, you begin to comprehend the enormity of the problem. The same institutional propaganda that initially fooled *you* still holds sway over millions and millions of minds. To unlock those minds, you must convince people to investigate ugly truths that, to them, seem ridiculous and

---

7 Source: Ed Griffin's interview with Norman Dodd: http://www.realityzone.com/hiddenagenda2.html
8 Source: Ed Griffin's interview with Norman Dodd: http://www.realityzone.com/hiddenagenda2.html

offensive. You have to overcome the fact that most people will be "unsympathetic to the purpose" of *any* investigation that challenges their deeply held beliefs.

Katherine Casey uncovered a criminal conspiracy that was so inherently immoral, and so at odds with popular perception, that few people would ever believe the story was true. And, since we don't have access to the documents she saw, healthy skepticism is perfectly reasonable. So, moving forward, let's assume that all we have to go on is a few general assertions:

1. Members of the Network believe they have a *right* to rule in secrecy.
2. By controlling policy and public perception, they have the *ability* to do so.
3. Because of their power within the political system, their crimes are rarely exposed and never properly punished.

Throughout the remainder of this book, I will prove that these three assertions are true.

Operation Northwoods

Like Katherine Casey, my world view changed forever when I stumbled across a document that I was never supposed to read. Coincidently, the secret document I saw also pertained to war; specifically, a plan to involve the United States in a war by convincing its citizens, its government, and its military that the nation had been attacked. The ugly truth (that the attack was to be an inside job) would be known only to a handful of individuals at the apex of power. Its success, like nearly everything the Network does, would rest on the exploitation of humanitarian impulses and the betrayal of public trust.

To really understand how easy it is for the Network to deceive a trusting public, let's begin with a thought experiment. Imagine the following hypothetical scenario:

The president of the United States appears on national television and announces that Iran has shot down a civilian airliner filled with two hundred American students. There are no survivors. The only thing that remains of the plane, its passengers, and its crew is the frantic tape of the pilot's final transmission: "Mayday, mayday, we're being tailed by an Iranian fighter...We need help up here and fast...Mayday, do you copy?," followed by the sound of an explosion, frantic screams, and then silence.

As the media plays the chilling audio over and over again (pausing periodically to interview grieving parents who have lost their children), the president assures the horrified and outraged public that the United States will act both swiftly and decisively. "We will not sit idly by as our nation's children are murdered in cold blood. This crazed and arrogant Iranian regime has been tolerated long enough, and it will now be brought to justice. I have instructed the secretary of defense to have a preliminary course of action prepared and on my desk by morning."

In this hypothetical scenario, very few people would have any desire whatsoever to stop the looming military confrontation. Quite the contrary—having been properly whipped into an emotional frenzy, they would cheer the "retaliatory" strike every step of the way. Even those who *did* question the wisdom and potential consequences of a war with Iran would be unlikely to speak up. They'd only be shouted down by an angry media-driven mob if they did. This is all basic human psychology; it is perfectly predictable. Equally predictable are the odds of anyone having any patience for an alternative narrative, especially a narrative that shifts blame from the well-established villain (Iran) to the well-meaning hero (the US government).

If you doubt this, just imagine some "conspiracy nut" standing up and stating the following: "It's all a lie! Iran is innocent! Our government was behind the whole thing! They loaded a civilian airliner with *fake* passengers, flew the plane to a secret location, unloaded the fake passengers, and replaced the original plane with a remote-controlled drone. They then had a *fake* Iranian fighter jet (it was really an American fighter painted to *look like* an Iranian fighter) chase after the remote-controlled drone. Then, they transmitted a fake "Mayday" signal from the drone just before blowing it up! It was all a setup so we could frame and attack Iran!"

What percentage of the trusting public could believe that *their* government would conspire to do something so utterly ridiculous and insane? Probably zero percent. Unless, of course, the trusting public's understanding of how "their government" actually operates was revealed to them via some shocking proof—some shocking proof that the "conspiracy nut" was right. Well, substitute Iran for Cuba, and you've got a nearly perfect description of the Northwoods Document.[9]

The Northwoods Document was an official US government plan to manipulate the people into supporting an unnecessary and illegal war. In the document, its authors propose many "pretexts" to achieve their aim: everything from *creating* a "terror campaign" in the United States to having covert US agents carry out attacks against US targets and then blaming Cuba for the attacks. It even speaks of completely fabricating an attack by using *fake* planes, *fake* passengers, remote-control drone aircraft, a *faked* mayday call, and a *faked* "shoot down." Sound unbelievable? It did to me as well, but then I read it for myself.

---

9 The "Top Secret" Northwoods Document is now declassified and is available for download at the George Washington University website: http://www.gwu.edu/~nsarchiv/news/20010430/

Here is the related text, excerpted directly from the Northwoods Document:

> As requested by Chief of Operations, Cuba Project, the Joint Chiefs of Staff are to indicate brief but precise description of pretexts which they consider would provide justification for US military intervention in Cuba...all projects are suggested within the time frame of the next few months.
>
> It is possible to create an incident which will demonstrate convincingly that a Cuban aircraft has attacked and shot down a chartered civil airliner... The passengers could be a group of college students off on a holiday or any grouping of persons with a common interest to support chartering a non-scheduled flight.
>
> a. An aircraft at Eglin Air Force Base would be painted and numbered as an exact duplicate for a civil registered aircraft belonging to a CIA proprietary organization...At a designated time, the duplicate would be substituted for the actual civil aircraft and would be loaded with selected passengers, all boarded under carefully prepared aliases. The actual registered aircraft would be converted to a drone.
>
> b. Take off times of the drone aircraft and the actual aircraft will be scheduled to allow a rendezvous south of Florida. From the rendezvous point the passenger-carrying aircraft will descend to minimum altitude and go directly into an auxiliary field at Eglin Air Force Base where arrangements will have been made to evacuate the passengers and return the aircraft to its original status. The drone aircraft meanwhile will continue to fly the filed flight plan. When over Cuba the drone will begin transmitting on the international distress frequency a 'May Day' message

stating he is under attack by Cuban MIG aircraft. The transmission will be interrupted by destruction of the aircraft which will be triggered by radio signal. This will allow ICAO radio stations in the Western Hemisphere to tell the US what has happened to the aircraft instead of the US trying to "sell" the incident.

Immediately prior to the proposal above, the document suggests having US military pilots threaten civilian aircraft with fake "MIG type aircraft." (This presumably would make a later "shoot down" that much more believable.)

An F-86 properly painted would convince air passengers that they saw a Cuban MIG, especially if the pilot of the transport were to announce such fact... reasonable copies of the MIG could be produced from US resources in about three months.

As noted, these plans were drafted in support of the larger Cuba Project, which was essentially a CIA-directed covert operation against Cuba. The Cuba Project contained many other equally immoral and dishonest proposals. One such proposal involved having the United States attack Jamaica and then blame the attack on Cuba.

Included in the nations the Joint Chiefs suggested as targets for covert attacks were Jamaica and Trinidad-Tobago. Since both were members of the British Commonwealth, the Joint Chiefs hoped that by secretly attacking them and then falsely blaming Cuba, the United States could incite the people of the United Kingdom into supporting a war against Castro.[10]

---

10 *Wikipedia*, Operation Northwoods:http://en.wikipedia.org/wiki/Operation_Northwoods

A plan was even put forward that suggested bribing a Cuban commander to launch an attack against the US military base at Guantanamo Bay. As James Bamford notes: "The act suggested—bribing a foreign nation to launch a violent attack on an American military installation—was treason."[11]

It's imperative to understand that covert operations of this nature rely on the *ignorance* of both the public *and* the vast majority of government and military personnel. (The whole point of a covert operation is to deceive; to get away with something you would otherwise be unable to get away with.) Regarding these and other proposals, a Department of Defense report stated clearly:

> If the decision should be made to set up a contrived situation it should be one in which participation by U.S. personnel is limited only to the most highly trusted covert personnel. This suggests the infeasibility of the use of military units for any aspect of the contrived situation.[12]

As part of the Cuba Project, Operation Northwoods was approved through the highest chain of command all the way up to the president of the United States. Fortunately, President Kennedy's opinion of the CIA and its tactics had already soured by the time the document hit his desk, and he rejected it. If he hadn't, this plan would have no doubt led to an unnecessary war and the death of many thousands based on total lies. Even worse, it could have easily led to a nuclear exchange with Russia and *millions dead*, based on lies.

Side Note: Kennedy's negative opinion of the Network-created CIA is summed up nicely in the following quote: "I

11 James Bamford, *Body of Secrets*, page 89
12 *Body of Secrets*, page 89

want to splinter the CIA into a thousand pieces and scatter it to the winds."[13] Many people, for good reason, believe the CIA played a direct role in both the murder of JFK and the cover-up that followed. That topic is beyond the scope of this book. However, just for reference, books like *JFK and the Unspeakable* do an excellent job of revealing the power struggle that emerged between Kennedy and his foreign policy "advisors" once he began moving the nation's foreign policy in an unapproved direction.

When I first read Operation Northwoods, I was still like Katherine Casey—terribly naïve. In my imaginary world, any individual who conspired to facilitate terrorist attacks against the United States[14] would be viewed as a terrorist and punished severely. Any group of *public servants* who set out to frame another nation for a crime it didn't commit, kill innocent people, and deceive the nation into an illegal war would be brought up on charges and thrown in prison for a very long time. But as I searched for information on how these conspirators were held accountable, I found nothing: no charges, no trials, no punishment.[15] It was as if deception, murder, and even *treason* were all acceptable just so long as the crimes were committed at the behest of the most powerful members of society. It didn't look anything like the "justice, freedom, and democracy" that I learned about in school. And as I dug deeper, it only got worse...much worse.

13 http://en.wikipedia.org/wiki/CIA_Kennedy_assassination_conspiracy_theory
14 "We could develop a Communist Cuban terror campaign in the Miami area, in other Florida cities and even in Washington."—Operation Northwoods
15 Some have argued that the Chairman of the Joint Chiefs of Staff, Lyman Lemnitzer, lost his job because of Operation Northwoods and therefore was "punished." But if Lemnitzer was being punished by our government for conspiring to carry out false-flag terror operations, it's odd that he was appointed "Supreme Allied Commander" of NATO. Hardly a demotion, his new post provided the opportunity to "fight communists" exactly the way he wanted. (Reference *Operation Gladio* in chapter 8 for more details.)

In 1998, Daniele Ganser was looking for a PhD research topic, and, against the advice of his friends and professors, he decided to tackle the gigantic task of unraveling "Operation Gladio." Beginning with a single document that proved the CIA and NATO *created* a secret terrorist army in Italy, he embarked on a four-year investigation that uncovered an additional *fifteen* secret armies in NATO countries and four more that were created in neutral countries.

There are many well-worn lies about the nature of our "leaders" and what they're capable of. The most obvious lie (to those who are paying attention) is that they respect national sovereignty, democracy, and "the will of the people." *Nothing* could be further from the truth, and Operation Gladio provides an excellent case in point. Gladio also underscores two key arguments that I've put forward in this book, which are:

1. The Network has mastered the art of pursuing its sovereignty-destruction project while maintaining the illusion of democracy, and
2. Its members operate above the moral and legislative laws that others are expected to abide by.

To address these points properly, we must first expand on some of the Network's handiwork prior to its implementation of Gladio following World War II. Unfortunately, because there is so much ground to cover, Gladio is going to have to wait until chapter 8.

World War I, the League of Nations, and Debt Traps

By manipulating the election of 1912, the Network brought Woodrow Wilson to power and effectively gained control of the "diplomatic machinery" of the United States. If, as Katherine Casey reported, the ultimate aim was to maneuver the United States into a war capable of altering "the life of an entire people," the Network was well on its way. All it needed now was the war itself, and, as luck would have it, Europe was already a powder keg that was primed and ready to explode. Henry Kissinger explains the political climate that preceded World War I this way:

> The astonishing aspect of the First World War is... that it took so long for it to happen...The statesmen of all the major countries had helped to construct [a] diplomatic doomsday mechanism.[16]
>
> The unholy mix of general political alliances and hair-trigger military strategies guaranteed a vast bloodletting...Foreign policy...now consisted of gambling on a single throw of the dice. A more mindless and technocratic approach to war would have been difficult to imagine.[17]

In June 1914, the so-called Black Hand[18] reached into Europe and set the "doomsday mechanism" into motion by assassinating Franz Ferdinand. The "vast bloodletting" followed shortly thereafter and, low and behold, the Network had its war. Now it was simply a matter of dragging the war on long enough for their carefully selected puppet (Woodrow Wilson) to sell "his" divinely inspired plan for US intervention and a New World Order.

With the carnage of World War I as a backdrop and with the father of propaganda, Edward Bernays, at his side,[19]

---

16 Henry Kissinger, *Diplomacy*, page 201
17 *Diplomacy*, page 206
18 The Black Hand was a secret society, established in the early 1900s http://en.wikipedia.org/wiki/Black_Hand_(Serbia)
19 "Bernays, working for the administration of Woodrow Wilson during World War I, was influential in promoting the idea that America's war efforts were primarily aimed at

Wilson began stirring support for the League of Nations that he'd been writing about since at least 1887.[20] Following "his" plan, the world would be led into a new and peaceful era where all nations, great and small, would be protected from unjust aggression and the violation of their sovereignty. Touting American principles, Wilson declared in May 1916:

> We believe these fundamental things: First, that every people has a right to choose the sovereignty under which they shall live...Second, that the small states of the world have a right to enjoy the same respect for their sovereignty and for their territorial integrity that great and powerful nations expect and insist upon. And, third, that the world has a right to be free from every disturbance of its peace that has its origin in aggression and disregard of the rights of peoples and nations.[21]

This lofty rhetoric, coupled with the outrage of a recent "surprise" attack on the "passenger liner" *Lusitania*[22], allowed the Network to steadily move the United States toward entering the European conflict. As it had done with the Federal Reserve System and income tax, the Network skillfully manipulated public opinion until it overcame the nation's strong antiwar sentiment. World War I, the people were assured, was a war that would end all wars. It would

'bringing democracy to all of Europe.'" http://en.wikipedia.org/wiki/Edward_Bernays
20 "Wilson himself had first written about world federation in 1887...he had contemplated 'a wide union...of governments joined with governments for the pursuit of common purpose.'" As quoted in *To End All Wars*, page 12
21 Woodrow Wilson, address delivered at the First Annual Assemblage of the League to Enforce Peace, May 27, 1916.http://www.presidency.ucsb.edu/ws/?pid=65391
22 In violation of international neutrality treaties, the *Lusitania* was being used to transport war materials while masquerading as a simple passenger liner. (The passengers were never informed of this fact.) We'll cover the case of the *Lusitania* in greater detail in the final chapter. For more information, see also: http://joeplummer.com/the_lusitania.html

"make the world safe for democracy" and lead mankind into a new era of respect for the rights of man. It was the duty of every liberty-loving citizen of the United States to support it, because no moral human could possibly oppose such ends.

Of course, if the utopian carrot wasn't enough, the Network also had a stick in its back pocket that it used to great effect. One week after a German torpedo sunk the *Lusitania*, killing nearly all Americans onboard, Professor Knock informs us:

> Americans barely had the chance to digest this assault [when] the British government released an official report on German atrocities, bearing the name...of Viscount James Bryce, the esteemed former Ambassador to the United States. [Bryce was a member of what Quigley referred to as the second generation of the Network's "Cecil Bloc."[23]] The crescendo of a systematic propaganda campaign to overcome American neutrality, this document catalogued in the most lurid detail some 1,200 alleged acts of barbarism and cruelty committed by German soldiers, primarily against Belgians—including the crucifixion and decapitation of prisoners of war, the gang rape and sexual mutilation of women, the hacking off of children's fingers for souvenirs, and the bayoneting of infants. Although much of it was later proved to be fictional...Germany would never fully recover from the revulsion that swept the United States.[24]

This carrot-and-stick propaganda campaign produced the desired result. The United States eventually entered

---

23 *The Anglo-American Establishment*, pages 30–31
24 *To End all Wars*, page 60

the war, and a constitutional abomination known as the Espionage Act was used to silence any remaining skeptics and dissenters. (Apparently, making the world "safe for democracy" meant demonizing and jailing US citizens who continued to voice their opposition. Opposition disrupted the campaign to establish "patriotic conformity,"[25] and so it could not be tolerated.) But the skeptics and dissenters were inevitably vindicated. At the war's end, the reality of power politics reared its ugly head. Quigley explains:

> The peoples of the victorious nations had taken to heart their wartime propaganda about the rights of small nations, making the world safe for democracy, and putting an end both to power politics and to secret diplomacy. These ideals had been given concrete form in Woodrow Wilson's Fourteen Points... the defeated powers had been promised...that the peace settlements would be negotiated and would be based on the Fourteen Points. When it became clear that **the settlements were to be imposed rather than negotiated...that the terms of the settlements had been reached by a process of secret negotiations from which the small nations had been excluded and in which power politics played a much larger role than the safety of democracy**, there was a revulsion of feeling against the treaties.[26]

Though the "peoples of the victorious nations" might have felt betrayed, members of the Network had plenty of

---

25 On page 133 of *To End all Wars*, Knock discusses some of the "ludicrous" aspects of the government's "campaign for patriotic conformity." For instance, German measles were renamed "Liberty measles," sauerkraut was renamed "Liberty cabbage," and German shepherds were renamed "police dogs." This snowballed into the banning of Brahms and Beethoven from concert halls, the removal and burning of German literature from some schools and public libraries, and even calls (by men like Theodore Roosevelt) to prohibit the teaching of the German language.
26 *Tragedy and Hope*, page 268

reasons to celebrate. Up to this point, they had achieved nearly every one of their aims: from the Wilson coup in 1912 to the Federal Reserve System and income tax; from maneuvering the United States into war, to creating a League of Nations that they would ultimately control. However, it was on this final point, the League of Nations, where the Network came up short.

When Wilson was forced to admit that the United States would have to cede sovereignty in order for the League to work, opposition within the US Senate began to grow.[27] In an attempt to overcome this opposition, he delivered yet another one of his messianic speeches in July 1919. The League of Nations, Wilson declared, was:

> The indispensable instrumentality for the maintenance of the new order...Dare we reject it and break the heart of the world?...The stage is set, the destiny disclosed. It has come about by no plan of our conceiving, but by the hand of God who led us into this way. We cannot turn back. We can only go forward, with lifted eyes and freshened spirit, to follow the vision. It was of this that we dreamed at our birth. America shall in truth show the way. The light streams upon the path ahead, and nowhere else.[28]

But no amount of lofty rhetoric or appeals to emotion would suffice. The League would clearly undermine US sovereignty, and Wilson was unable to rally enough support within the Senate to overcome this objection. In November 1919, after months of debate, the US Senate voted *not* to join.[29] However, this isn't to suggest that the Network's efforts had been in vain. A great deal of money

---

27 *To End All Wars*, pages 232, 233
28 *To End All Wars*, pages 251, 252
29 http://www.senate.gov/reference/reference_item/Versailles.htm

had been made during the war, competing empires had been destroyed, power had been consolidated, and dozens of nations *had* joined the League. The Network simply had some more work to do within the United States, and "more work" it did. Aside from increasing its control over government using the Inquiry, the CFR, and other well-connected instruments, it also began increasing its financial control with its new monetary weapon, the Federal Reserve System.

Stealing Gold and Creating Debt

After World War I, the Federal Reserve began artificially inflating the US dollar supply. Quigley informs us that this was done, in large part, to allow gold to be drained from the United States (for Britain's benefit) without triggering a corresponding reduction in the number of US dollars in circulation.[30] The newly printed Fed money flowed into the stock market, inflated the bubble of the Roaring Twenties, and inevitably led to the stock market crash of 1929 and the economic devastation of the Great Depression. (This too helped to "alter the life of an entire people.")

Making economic matters worse, Britain went off the gold standard completely in 1931, and this predictably intensified the depletion of US gold. (Nations that could no longer redeem their paper receipts for gold in Britain now turned to the United States.) Since the US was "the only gold standard country with gold coins still circulating," gold poured out of the country. Additionally, concerned US citizens began redeeming large quantities of *their* dollars for gold too, and "the US banking system began to collapse."[31]

This pressure on the banking system continued until 1933 when the Network convinced President Roosevelt

---

30 *Tragedy and Hope*, page 342
31 *Tragedy and Hope*, pages 349, 350

(FDR) to confiscate US citizens' gold and hand it over to the Federal Reserve.[32] By making it illegal for US citizens to redeem their dollars in gold, the Federal Reserve (in cooperation with policy makers within the federal government) could now begin printing ever-larger piles of debt money while increasing their own power in the process. As covered in chapter 4, a heavily indebted government is much easier to control than one that is financially sound. Even Quigley admits that making gold illegal in the United States was not necessary. He states that it was done "in order to pursue a policy of price inflation...it was not made necessary by the American international financial position."[33] It's also worth noting that Mandell House, more than twenty years after advising Woodrow Wilson, was an advisor to FDR as well.

If the Network *always* seeks to trap nations in debt (it does), then a review of the growth in US federal debt should be instructive (and it is). In the twenty years *prior* to Wilson's election, the amount of debt the federal government owed increased by just $1.3 billion. In the twenty years *after* Wilson's election, the amount of debt the federal government owed increased by nearly $20 billion.[34] (This massive increase in debt occurred *despite* the additional revenue provided by the 1913 personal income tax.) But even this $20 billion increase was just a drop in the bucket; fast forward to just after FDR's presidency, and the federal debt had increased by more than $240 billion. And in 2012, it had increased by more than $16,000 billion.

This information on government debt is vitally important because it plays a major role in the Network's destruction of national sovereignty. Financial warfare is *essential,*

---

32 http://en.wikipedia.org/wiki/Executive_Order_6102
33 *Tragedy and Hope*, page 350
34 http://www.usgovernmentdebt.us

and the basic recipe for conquering a nation financially can be summed up in two simple steps:

1. Create shortfalls in government revenue. (Either by increasing the amount of money a government spends, decreasing the amount of money a government collects, or both.)
2. Create loans out of thin air to "help" the "leaders" cover their spending shortfalls without correcting the underlying financial imbalance.

As payments on mounting debt create greater and greater shortfalls, and as annual spending continues to increase unabated, larger and more frequent loans become necessary to bridge the gap. This accelerates the rate at which the national debt grows and, before long, even powerful nations will find themselves utterly dependent on a constant flow of newly borrowed funds to cover their expenses.

Once a nation has been trapped in this way, the Network can simply adjust the financial spigot according to the level at which its desires are being met. If a government wants to maintain vital services, social order, and ultimately its own power, it will do what the Network wants (regardless of the will of the people). If the government refuses, the flow of money will be cut and won't be restored until "more acceptable" leaders assume control. And as we'll cover in the next chapter, "acceptable" has nothing to do with how the new leaders treat the citizens that live beneath them.

CHAPTER 7
Sink the League—Raise the Fascists

"The New World Order cannot happen without U.S.
participation, as we are the most significant single
component...there will be a New World Order, and it will
force the United States to change its perceptions."
—Henry Kissinger[1]

Around the time it became clear the United States wouldn't
join the League of Nations, the Network began the process
of undermining the organization. Quigley seems perplexed
by this, especially regarding its erosion of provisions within
the League that, although harsh, were meant to restrain
dangerous groups that still held power in post-WWI Germany. On page 232 of *The Anglo-American Establishment*, he
writes:

> Philip Kerr was...at the very center of the Milner
> Group. His violent Germanophobia...and his evi-
> dent familiarity with the character of the Germans...
> *should have* made the Treaty of Versailles very accept-
> able to him and his companions, or, if not, unaccept-
> able on grounds of excessive *leniency*. Instead, Kerr...
> and the whole inner core of the Milner Group began
> a campaign to undermine the treaty, the League

---

1 http://en.wikipedia.org/wiki/New_world_order_(politics)

of Nations, and the whole peace settlement...The Milner Group...began their program of appeasement and revision of the settlement as early as 1919. Why did they do this?

Quigley answers his own question via a process that he admits involves "a certain amount of conjecture." First, he argues that the well-meaning men of the Network had simply mistaken the true nature (and actual identity) of those who continued to rule Germany after its defeat in 1918. *If only they had known* these facts, they wouldn't have pursued the flawed policy of appeasement, and "there need never have been a Second World War." In Quigley's defense, he does mention that:

> The Milner Group did not see...because they did not want to see.
> The Milner Group knew that [the true powers in Germany] were cooperating with the reactionaries to suppress all democratic and enlightened elements in Germany and to help the forces of despotism.[2]

Quigley then goes on to describe a series of deceptive actions taken by the Group (where they *pretended* to support positions that they actually opposed, and *pretended* to oppose positions that they actually supported), and the reader is left wondering how anyone could possibly decipher what the Group was *truly* thinking or trying to accomplish. For instance, he states that the "economic expert" within the Milner Group decided that the best way to *help Germany* become an upstanding member of Western civilization would be to have the United States begin loaning Germany money.[3] But if the Group *knew* the "forces of despotism" were being empowered,

---

2 *The Anglo-American Establishment*, pages 234 and 235
3 *The Anglo-American Establishment*, page 235

and assuming they did not want to strengthen those forces, why would they begin extending "concessions to the Germans without any attempt to purge Germany of its vicious elements and without any guarantee that those concessions would not be used against everything the Group held dear"?[4]

One could reasonably argue that the loans offered to help Germany were simply part of a surreptitious financial warfare strategy. On pages 308 and 309 of *Tragedy and Hope*, Quigley describes an $800 million loan to Germany, known as the Dawes Plan, this way:

> The Dawes Plan, which was largely a J. P. Morgan production, was drawn up by an international committee of financial experts…Germany paid reparations for five years under the Dawes Plan (1924–1929) and owed more at the end than it had owed at the beginning…It is worthy of note that this system was set up by the international bankers and that the subsequent lending of other people's money to Germany was profitable to these bankers…With these American loans, Germany was able to rebuild her industrial system to make it the second best in the world by a wide margin…The only things wrong with the system were (a) that it would collapse as soon as the United States ceased to lend, and (b) in the meantime debts were merely being shifted from one account to another and no one was really getting any nearer to solvency…Nothing was settled by all this, but the international bankers sat in heaven, under a rain of fees and commissions.

This sounds like a pretty run-of-the-mill debt trap; the bankers get rich as a targeted nation gets buried in

---

4 *The Anglo-American Establishment*, page 238

inescapable debt. However, this particular nation was using the borrowed money to rebuild its capacity for war. Backed with an industrial system that ranked second in the world "by a wide margin," the idea that Germany's "vicious elements" would simply accept having their funding cut (once they were militarily strong enough to *seize* new resources) is pretty farfetched. The Network was wise enough to know that its actions were creating a potentially dangerous military force in Europe, one that couldn't be easily contained via economic sanctions alone. So, does this mean that it wanted Germany, vicious elements and all, to become strong again? In a word, yes. Quigley eventually settles on this conclusion and then offers an explanation for why the Network decided to undermine the League of Nations.

After the United States refused to join the League, members of the Milner Group concluded that their best option in Europe was to revive Germany and use it as a weapon against both France and Russia. But before this balance-of-power strategy could be implemented, the League of Nations would have to be destroyed. (As it was written, the League would not only interfere with Germany's ability to rearm, but it would also interfere with Germany's ability to violate the sovereignty of neighboring nations.)

> The aim of the Milner Group through the period from 1920 to 1938 was the same: to maintain the balance of power in Europe by building up Germany against France and Russia; to increase Britain's weight in that balance...to refuse any commitments (especially any commitments through the League of Nations, and above all any commitments to aid France)...to drive Germany eastward against Russia if either or both of these two powers became a threat to the peace of Western Europe.

> From 1921 onward, the Milner Group and the British Government...did all they could to lighten the reparations burden on Germany and to prevent France from using force to collect reparations.[5]

Remember, France had only survived German aggression during WWI because Britain, the United States, Russia, and Italy had come to her aid. As the Network's secret policy to remilitarize Germany began taking shape, the French became progressively more alarmed. Quigley writes that France "sought in vain one alternative after another" to guarantee its security and to keep Germany down, but "all of these efforts were blocked by the machinations of the Milner Group."[6] When, at the behest of the Network, Britain blocked the Geneva Protocol in 1924, this finally sparked outrage around the world. True to form, the Network simply turned the outrage to its own advantage.

> There was an outburst of public sentiment against the selfish and cold-blooded action...As a result of this feeling, which was widespread throughout the world, the Group determined to give the world the *appearance* of a guarantee to France. This was done in the Locarno Pacts...In reality, the agreements gave France nothing while they gave Britain a veto over French fulfillment of her alliances...if Germany moved east against Czechoslovakia [or] Poland... and if France attacked Germany's western frontier in support of Czechoslovakia or Poland, as her alliances bound her to do, Great Britain, Belgium and Italy might be bound by the Locarno Pacts to come to the aid of Germany.[7]

---

5 *The Anglo-American Establishment*, pages 240, 241
6 *The Anglo-American Establishment*, page 261
7 *The Anglo-American Establishment*, page 264

This, of course, wasn't the last time the Network betrayed world opinion and public trust in pursuit of its disastrous European agenda. Quigley uses the term "dual policy" to describe additional deceptions that were employed in the run-up to World War II. ("Dual policy" can be summarized as *pretending* to honor the "will of the people" publicly, while continuing to pursue antithetical policies behind the scenes.) These deliberate deceptions not only empowered men like Adolf Hitler in Germany, they also empowered the fascist regimes of Benito Mussolini in Italy and Francisco Franco in Spain.

Benito Mussolini

According to Quigley, "one of the most astonishing examples of British 'dual policy' in the appeasement period" occurred when Britain allowed Mussolini to conquer and seize Ethiopia. At the time, the British public was still operating under the assumption that the League of Nations was *created* to protect the sovereignty of weaker nations. As such, a poll of 11.5 million British citizens found that more than 11 million felt Ethiopia should be protected from Italian aggression under the League, 10 million supported economic sanctions against Italy, and more than 6.5 million supported military sanctions if necessary.[8]

Prior to this poll, the ruling party in Britain had expressed its indifference regarding the fate of Ethiopia. *After* the poll, it changed its tune completely. All of a sudden "collective security" and the League of Nations were of the utmost importance in British foreign policy, and new candidates were trotted out to ride the "wave of public support for collective security."[9] The prime minister and foreign secretary were replaced to "make people believe that

8 *Tragedy and Hope*, pages 573, 574
9 *Tragedy and Hope*, page 574

the past program of appeasement would be reversed,"[10] and Quigley provides an example of how the new foreign secretary (Samuel Hoare), fulfilled his part in the deception.

> In September, Hoare made a vigorous speech at Geneva in which he pledged Britain's support of collective security to stop the Italian aggression against Ethiopia. The public did not know that he had stopped off in Paris en route to Geneva to arrange a secret deal by which Italy would be given two-thirds of Ethiopia.[11]
>
> While publicly supporting collective security and sanctions against Italian aggression, the government privately negotiated to destroy the League and to yield Ethiopia to Italy. They were completely successful in this secret policy...In the process they gave the League of Nations, the collective-security system, and the political stability of central Europe their death wounds.[12]
>
> The consequences of the Ethiopian fiasco were of the greatest importance. Mussolini was much strengthened in Italy [and, as a result of the deceptive "collective-security" election promises] The Conservative Party in England was entrenched in office for a decade, during which it carried out its policy of appeasement and waged the resulting war.[13]

Quigley doesn't say much about how Mussolini was initially helped into his position of power. A passing comment on page 242 of *Tragedy and Hope* simply states that

---

10 *Tragedy and Hope,* page 492
11 *Tragedy and Hope,* pages 492, 493
12 *Tragedy and Hope,* page 574
13 *Tragedy and Hope,* page 576

Mussolini received funding from the Entente governments during World War I, and this funding eventually paved the way for his "unprincipled career which ultimately made him dictator of Italy." However, Quigley *does* spend a good amount of time describing the rise of General Francisco Franco in Spain.

Francisco Franco

If you'd like to read a short section of *Tragedy and Hope* that covers pretty much every filthy aspect of political power (widespread corruption, gross negligence, secret deals, exploitation of the population, horrendous military waste that benefits a select few, assassinations, overthrowing representative government, etc.), then read pages 586 to 604. In those pages, Quigley covers everything from the Spanish-American War of 1898 to the Franco dictatorship that took over Spain in 1939. Though it's far from uplifting, it's definitely an interesting section of the book.

Here, we only need to cover the Franco revolution and his rise to power. On this topic, Quigley first discusses an agreement between Mussolini and "conspirators" seeking to overthrow the Spanish government. He states that Mussolini "promised arms, money, and diplomatic support to the revolutionary movement and gave the conspirators a first-installment payment of 1,500,000 pesetas, 10,000 rifles, 10,000 grenades, and 200 machine guns."[14] So, by this point, the consequences of Britain's appeasement of Mussolini have begun to spill over. (By *appeasing* the fascist regime of Mussolini, *Mussolini* gained the freedom to empower another fascist regime in neighboring Spain.)

When the Spanish government discovered that General Francisco Franco was conspiring to seize control of the

---

14 *Tragedy and Hope*, page 594

country, it attempted to derail the plot by transferring him to the Canary Islands. But this was little more than a temporary setback. A "well-known editor" in England was able to retrieve Franco from exile, fly him to Morocco, and even supply another fifty machine guns and half a million rounds of ammunition for the coup. After arriving in Morocco, Franco requested and received some assistance from Hitler as well, and by early August 1936, the fascist revolution was well underway.[15] But the Spanish government proved very resilient.

Despite assistance from Italy, Germany, and even Portugal, Franco's initial coup was only partially successful. The German secretary of foreign affairs noted as much near the end of August when he wrote: "It is not to be expected that the Franco Government can hold out for long...without large-scale support from outside."[16] It appeared as if the Spanish government would soon defeat Franco and the rebels. But that was *before* Britain and France entered the equation with a so-called "nonintervention" agreement.

As written, the nonintervention agreement should have helped the Spanish government because it prohibited Italy, Germany, and Portugal from providing any more assistance to Franco and the rebels. Also, the agreement made it *seem* like Britain was trying to honor the will of its citizens. (By about 8 to 1, the British public supported the Spanish government and opposed the rebels seeking to overthrow it.) The reality, of course, was quite different. Quigley writes that Britain was neither "fair nor neutral" in the way that it enforced the nonintervention agreement, and that Britain engaged "in large-scale violations of international law" (to the benefit of Franco and the rebels), during the course of the Spanish Civil War. He adds:

15 *Tragedy and Hope*, page 597
16 *Tragedy and Hope*, page 598

The nonintervention agreement, as practiced, was neither an aid to peace nor an example of neutrality, but was clearly enforced in such a way as to give aid to the rebels and place all possible obstacles in the way of the [Spanish] government suppressing the rebellion.

This attitude of the British government could not be admitted publicly, and every effort was made to picture the actions of the Nonintervention Committee as one of evenhanded neutrality. In fact, the activities of this committee were used to **throw dust in the eyes of the world**, and especially in the eyes of the British public.

Britain's attitude was so devious that it can hardly be untangled, although the results are clear enough. The chief result was that in Spain a Left government friendly to France was replaced by a Right government unfriendly to France and deeply obligated to Italy and Germany.

When the war ended, much of Spain was wrecked, at least 450,000 Spaniards had been killed…and an unpopular military dictatorship had been imposed on Spain as a result of the actions of non-Spanish forces.[17]

Franco "went on to become the longest-ruling dictator in European history." During his reign, he repealed civil liberties, violently oppressed dissenting voices, and murdered tens of thousands of his political opponents. In power from 1939 until his death in 1975, Franco's funeral was attended not only by fellow Network-supported dictators, but also by such Network royalty as US vice president Nelson Rockefeller.[18]

---

17 *Tragedy and Hope*, in order: pages 603, 602, and 604
18 http://en.wikipedia.org/wiki/Francisco_Franco

Adolf Hitler

Although a great deal has been written about Adolf Hitler, you'll rarely find any mention of the Network or its role in the rise of Nazi Germany. The unspeakable human suffering of World War II can hardly be imagined, let alone captured with words, and so there will be no attempt to do so here. Rather, I'll simply provide a few final details about the tactics and policies (enacted by a handful of men) that made the Nazi regime and World War II a reality.

After successfully facilitating the remilitarization of Germany, the Network continued moving forward with its plan. That *plan* included the liquidation of Austria, Czechoslovakia and Poland. However, to assure success, another obstacle to German power had to be removed: France had to be ejected from the western German Rhineland so that German troops could reoccupy the area. On this, Quigley writes:

> It would be too complicated a story to narrate here the methods by which France was persuaded to yield...It is enough to point out that France was persuaded to withdraw her troops [from the Rhineland] in 1930 rather than 1935 as a result of what she believed to be concessions made to her.[19]

Here Quigley explains the importance of maintaining a demilitarized Rhineland. Once Germany fortified this area (in violation of the Treaty of Versailles), it could move east into the countries "marked for liquidation" with less fear of a French attack on Germany's western border.[20]

---

19 *The Anglo-American Establishment,* page 266
20 *The Anglo-American Establishment,* page 272

The Rhineland and a zone fifty kilometers wide...
were to be permanently demilitarized and any violation of this could be regarded as a hostile act by the
signers of the treaty. This meant that any **German
troops or fortifications were excluded from this
area forever. This was the most important clause of
the Treaty of Versailles.** So long as it remained in
effect...the economic backbone of Germany's ability
to wage warfare, was exposed to a quick French military thrust from the west, and Germany could not
threaten France or move eastward against Czechoslovakia or Poland if France objected.[21]

The French undoubtedly understood the strategic danger of a German-occupied Rhineland when they left the
area, but they falsely believed that the Locarno Pacts would
prevent Germany from moving troops back in. According
to Quigley, this was just another one of the Network's deceptions. The Locarno Pacts were intentionally drawn up with
loopholes that would allow Britain to "escape the necessity
of fulfilling her guarantee..." Quigley adds:

> As a matter of fact, when Hitler did violate the
> Locarno agreements by remilitarizing the Rhine-
> land in March of 1936, the Milner Group and their
> friends did not even try to evade their obligation by
> slipping through a loophole...they simply dishon-
> ored their agreement.[22]

With Hitler's Germany successfully returned to the
Rhineland, and with the stage set for his conquest of Austria, Czechoslovakia, and Poland, the Network began deal-
ing with the final obstacle that stood in its way: public

---

21 *Tragedy and Hope*, pages 277, 278
22 *The Anglo-American Establishment*, page 265

opinion. Clearly, the British government couldn't admit its decision to feed three sovereign nations to the Nazis, so to keep public outcry to a minimum, it began manipulating and terrorizing citizens into accepting Hitler's actions.

> The chief task of the Milner Group was to see that this devouring process was done no faster than public opinion in Britain could accept, [and also] to soften up the prospective victims so that they would not resist the process and thus precipitate a war.[23]
>
> [The British government created fear by] steadily exaggerating Germany's armed might and belittling their own, by calculated indiscretions (like the statement...that there were no real antiaircraft defenses in London), by constant hammering at the danger of an overwhelming air attack without warning, by building ostentatious and quite useless air-raid trenches in the streets and parks of London, and by insisting through daily warnings that everyone must be fitted with a gas mask immediately (although the danger of a gas attack was nil). In this way, the government put London into a panic.[24]

As noted, this tactic of inciting panic (which was gradually built up from 1935 through 1939), was also used on the "prospective victims" of Nazi aggression. Britain applied intense political pressure on the countries that were expected to yield their sovereignty to Hitler, placing special emphasis on an exaggerated account of Germany's military strength and blunt declarations that the victims would be on their own if they chose to resist Hitler's plans. They were led

---

23 *The Anglo-American Establishment*, page 273
24 *Tragedy and Hope*, page 584, with additional details regarding the propaganda on page 622

to believe that resistance was futile. They were assured that Britain would *not* intervene on their behalf.

Following this formula, Austria was the first country to fall without a fight. After its annexation, "those who had opposed the Nazis were murdered or enslaved, the Jews were plundered and abused, and extravagant honors were paid to the Nazi gangsters who had been disturbing Austria for years."[25] Apparently, all of this was OK with the Network, because it immediately began working on the next target; Czechoslovakia.

> Within two weeks of Hitler's annexation of Austria, Britain was moving. It was decided to put pressure on the Czechs to make concessions to the Germans... All this was justified by the arguments that Czechoslovakia, in a war with Germany, would be smashed immediately.[26]

On pages 625 through 639 of *Tragedy and Hope,* you'll discover the truly disgraceful step-by-step process that ultimately destroyed Czechoslovakia. Using a combination of "merciless secret pressure," threats, and deception, the Network eventually wore down its opposition and achieved its goal. Though the story is too long to adequately summarize here, suffice to say: one of the most "democratic, prosperous and best-administered" post-WWI nations *also* fell to the Nazis without a fight, and the predictable consequences followed soon after.

> The anti-Nazi refugees...were rounded up by the Prague government and handed over to the Germans to be destroyed...Germany was supreme in central Europe, and any possibility of curtailing that

---

25 *Tragedy and Hope,* page 625
26 *Tragedy and Hope,* page 627

power either by a joint policy of the Western Powers with the Soviet Union and Italy or by finding any openly anti-German resistance in central Europe itself was ended. Since this is exactly what Chamberlain [the British Prime Minister] and his friends had wanted, they should have been satisfied.[27]

Satisfied or not, the issue of liquidating Poland remained on the list of things to do, and this is where the Network's ability to manipulate public opinion began to lose ground. Following Hitler's final annexation of Czechoslovakia and the Memel region of Lithuania, citizens turned downright hostile toward any continued appeasement of the Nazis. Hitler's actions had opened their eyes "to the fact that appeasement was merely a kind of slow suicide, and quite incapable of satisfying the appetites of aggressors who were insatiable."

This final realization might have been an epiphany for the average citizen, but "Hitler's real ambitions were quite clear to most men in government" long before his brazen actions in Czechoslovakia, and they "were made clear to the rest during the crisis." Nevertheless, appeasement and concessions to Hitler continued, only now they continued in secrecy.[28] There is no mystery to how this tragic story ends.

Hitler became progressively more belligerent and impatient, insisting on his right to use force to acquire his desires. According to Quigley, this is the only reason the Network finally turned on him. (It seems they had no problem with Hitler murdering and ruthlessly oppressing people; he had done that from day one of his 1933 German coup. Their main issue, assuming Quigley is correct, was that he refused to be more *diplomatic* in the way he gained control of the sovereign nations that he intended to oppress.)

---

27 *Tragedy and Hope*, pages 638, 639
28 *Tragedy and Hope*, pages 641, 642

In the shadow of the League of Nations and world opinion, overt Nazi violations of national sovereignty put increasing pressure on the Network's Western puppets. When Hitler violently attacked Poland in 1939, this finally forced the Network's hand.[29] Thus began a six-year-long "tide of aggression" and "cold-blooded savagery" on a scale that had never been seen before. Civilian deaths far exceeded those of combatants, and many of both "were killed without any military justification" whatsoever. For instance, in the 1939 Battle of Poland, 3.9 *million* Polish civilians "were executed, or murdered in the ghetto."[30] As for the *total* number of civilians killed during the war (in all nations combined), that number has been continually revised upward since the initial release of *Tragedy and Hope*. According to Wikipedia:

> Civilians killed totaled from 38 to 55 million, including 13 to 20 million from war-related disease and famine. Total military dead: from 22 to 25 million, including deaths in captivity of about 5 million prisoners of war.[31]

Accepting the two lowest estimates above, we arrive at sixty million dead. To put that enormous number in perspective, sixty million people taken from the United States would have wiped out nearly half of the 1940 US population. This horrific body count is made even more disturbing when you realize that those most responsible for orchestrating World War II likely walked away with *zero* casualties.

And, once again, the same Network that nurtured and facilitated an unspeakable global disaster profited

---

29 This view is based on Quigley's narrative. It is equally possible that the Network had planned, from the start, to instigate another global conflagration and use it to secure its greater objectives.
30 *Tragedy and Hope*, page 661
31 http://en.wikipedia.org/wiki/World_War_II_casualties

handsomely. Not just financially via the billions *earned* and mountains of debt added to government balance sheets, but more so politically. That is, where the Network failed to secure US participation in its League of Nations scheme following WWI, it succeeded in securing US participation in its second global-government scheme (the United Nations) following WWII. This essentially destroyed the problem of American "isolationism." With that out of the way, the United States has done the heavy lifting in the Network's sovereignty-destruction project ever since.

From Global *Government* to Global *Governance*

Quigley claims that the Network's first global-government scheme (the League of Nations) was never *really* meant to be used as an instrument of "collective security" or impede sovereignty in any meaningful way. I'd be remiss if I didn't address this foolish assertion. Though Quigley bases his claim on the statements of men within the Network, he again fails to weigh their propensity for deception. Reading between the lines, a much more believable argument emerges. Here, I'll briefly summarize that argument.

If the United States *had agreed* to join the League of Nations after WWI, the Network would have gladly begun using the military might, financial resources, and good name of the United States in pursuit of its global objectives. "Obligations" under the League's *collective-security* agreement would have been invoked when convenient, and ignored when inconvenient. Contrary to Quigley's claim, it isn't that a "League of Coercion" wasn't desired by the Network; it's that such a league *required* US participation to work. In support of this assertion, consider the following:

1. The majority of the Network's statements *opposing* "collective security" came *after* it was clear that the United States would not join the League and, therefore, would not participate in enforcement. This is when the Network began seriously undermining the League; this is when it decided to embark on its policy of so-called "appeasement." In other words: the Network could not demand that the British protect the sovereignty of nations that it had already decided to allow Hitler, Mussolini, and Spanish rebels to violate. To do so would only turn British power *against* the Network's own aims.

2. The Network was present every step of the way during the drafting of the League of Nations. It was present every step of the way for the world-wide propaganda campaign in support of the League of Nations. It had every opportunity to speak out against objectionable language or "obligations" under collective security. But again, meaningful opposition didn't come until after the United States refused to join. Why? Well, one quote states that the failure to secure the United States' participation presented "a very serious problem for the British Empire" because, by joining the League without the United States, Britain had "undertaken great obligations" that it now had to "in honesty and self-regard, revise."[32] Another quote states that once the United States rejected the League "the keystone was taken out of the whole arch of any League of Coercion."[33]

3. There *are* some specific Network statements against the League serving as "world government," but even these are hedged with qualifiers like "it could be a world government" *if* given the power to tax citizens

---

32 *The Anglo-American Establishment*, page 254
33 *The Anglo-American Establishment*, page 271

and if it "represented" those citizens instead of representing states.[34] (The irony of this sentiment coming from men who set out to destroy "representation," in favor of fascist regimes, is hard to miss.) Another quote simply states that the Milner Group sought to "prevent influential people from using the League as an instrument of world government *before* popular opinion was *ready* for a world government."[35]

4. Quigley himself admits that "certain phrases or implications were introduced…which could be taken to indicate that the League might have been intended to be used as a real instrument of collective security, that it might have involved some minute limitation of sovereignty, that sanctions might under certain circumstances be used to protect the peace."[36] He even references a quote that explicitly states "interference with national sovereignty," including "international coercion" would be *necessary* if a nation refused to cooperate with the League during its ninety-day dispute period,[37] but he dismisses this in favor of accepting, what I believe was, propaganda aimed at skeptical statesmen. (Specifically, propaganda aimed at skeptical *US* statesmen.)

By now, admittedly, this is a moot point. The League of Nations was replaced by the post-WWII United Nations, and there is absolutely no question regarding how the UN and its related agencies (like the IMF and World Bank) have been used to violate national sovereignty. But even *this* fact is now fading in relevance, because the Network is seeking to replace the UN with something even more powerful.

---

34 *The Anglo-American Establishment*, page 252
35 *The Anglo-American Establishment*, page 259
36 *The Anglo-American Establishment*, pages 248, 249
37 *The Anglo-American Establishment*, page 251

Quoting from a 2008 CFR program entitled "International Institutions and Global Governance—World Order in the 21st Century":[38]

> The Council on Foreign Relations (CFR) has launched a comprehensive five-year program on international institutions and global governance. The purpose of this cross-cutting initiative is to explore the institutional requirements for world order in the twenty-first century. The undertaking recognizes that the architecture of global governance—largely reflecting the world as it existed in 1945—has not kept pace with fundamental changes in the international system.

A twelve-page summary of the project states that "the program draws on the resources of the CFR's David Rockefeller Studies Program" and its purpose is to offer "recommendations" to US policymakers about how to improve the performance of "global governance mechanisms."

In order for the United States to assume its proper role in the emerging world order, it targets certain issues that must be dealt with. Issues like US adherence to "constitutional traditions," "sovereign prerogatives," and "the separation of powers...which gives Congress a critical voice in the ratification of treaties and endorsement of global institutions" all serve to complicate the United States' ability to assume its "new international obligations." Yes, you read that correctly. The Constitution, separation of powers, Congress's voice in the ratification of treaties, and, of course, sovereignty itself are all listed as *problems* that must be overcome.

---

38 http://www.cfr.org/content/thinktank/CFR_Global%20_Governance_%20 Program.pdf

For those versed in the cynical ways of the Network, the pretexts offered for circumventing constitutional limitations in favor of embracing Network-directed "global governance" will surely make the blood boil. Here are just a few:

1. "Managing the global economy" (a pretext for further consolidation and control of the world's monetary system)
2. The recently rebranded "climate change" (a pretext for funding the Network's global government *and* for centralizing control over the one thing no nation can survive without: *energy*)
3. "Preventing and responding to violent conflict" ("violent conflict" is often *caused* by the Network itself and then used as a pretext for intervention and interference with national sovereignty)

However, the pretext that jumps out the most, the one that actually mocks the reader's intelligence, is the "struggle against al-Qaeda and affiliated organizations."

The Network has funded, trained, and armed terrorists in pursuit of its global objectives for decades. This *fact* can be easily verified by researching any number of historical events. Whether it's Operation Ajax in 1953, or Operation Cyclone in 1979, or Bosnia and Kosovo in the 1990s, or Libya and Syria in 2011 and 2013, respectively...in each case the *terrorists* found aid and comfort by turning to the West.

None of this is mentioned, of course, in the CFR white paper. However, it does admit that the rise of transnational terrorist organizations has "forced the United States and its allies to tolerate some sacrifice of national sovereignty [and] reconcile distinct constitutional and legal traditions." Rather convenient.

In the final chapters, we'll delve deeper into Network-sponsored acts of terrorism, which are often referred to as "false flag" operations. Keep in mind: although these acts are directed by Western-government institutions, the *vast majority* of the military, political leadership, and civilian population is never told the truth about what "their government" is doing.

CHAPTER 8
False and Designing Men

In the previous chapter, we touched on one of the more devious ways that leaders can manipulate the public: they can choose to implement a *dual policy* (that is, a policy of publicly *pretending* to honor the will of the people, while simultaneously doing everything possible to evade it). By any reasonable measure, dual policies constitute an egregious betrayal of democratic principles and public trust. They also reveal the deeply dishonest nature of the ruling class. However, dual policies are *not* the most effective or the most immoral way to manipulate the public. For that, we must turn to the false-flag operation.

The term "false flag" usually describes a deadly or immoral act that is planned and carried out by one group but is made to *appear* as if it was planned and carried out by another. Adolf Hitler's Operation Himmler provides a good example. It consisted of a series of false-flag operations, each designed to create the appearance of Polish aggression against Germany. One way the Nazis achieved this was by taking prisoners from concentration camps, dressing them in German uniforms, and then killing them on the Polish frontier.[1] These "dead Germans" were later used by Hitler as a justification for attacking Poland in 1939.

---

1 *Tragedy and Hope*, page 657

While false flags are commonly used as a pretext for war, they can also be used by leaders to justify silencing dissent, suspending civil liberties, and seizing additional power. Again, we can turn to Adolf Hitler for an example. Prior to the German election of March 5, 1933, the Nazi Party had done all it could to weaken and disrupt opposing political parties, but despite their best efforts, it appeared as if the Nazis would still face stiff competition at the polls. Here, Quigley describes how they dealt with this problem:

> Under circumstances which are still mysterious, a plot was worked out to burn the Reichstag building and blame the Communists...After the building was set on fire...the government at once arrested four Communists, including the party leader in the Reichstag. The day following the fire [Hindenburg, the president of Germany] signed a decree suspending all civil liberties and giving the government power to invade any personal privacy, including the right to search private homes or confiscate property. At once all Communist members of the Reichstag, as well as thousands of others, were arrested...The true story of the Reichstag fire was kept secret only with difficulty. Several persons who knew the truth...were murdered in March and April to prevent their circulating the true story. Most of the Nazis who were in on the plot were murdered by Goring during the "blood purge" of June 30, 1934.[2]

Both Operation Himmler and the plot to burn the Reichstag provide straightforward examples of false-flag operations, but other variations do exist. For instance, sometimes the act of aggression and subsequent casualties

---

2 *Tragedy and Hope*, pages 437, 438

are completely fabricated. If you recall from chapter 6, Operation Northwoods offered this type of false flag as one potential option. The proposal involved an elaborate scheme using a remote-controlled drone aircraft and fake cockpit transmissions to make it appear as if Cuba had shot down a US civilian airliner filled with students on vacation. (After being widely reported in the media, this nonevent could have then been used as a pretext for going to war with Cuba.) Northwoods also proposed other common false-flag variations like provoking the enemy and then *allowing* them to successfully attack (known as a "stand down" false flag) and also *creating* an enemy, in the form of a terrorist group, and then using the subsequent "terror attacks" as a pretext for going to war.

Although Operation Northwoods was endorsed by the highest-ranking officer in the US armed forces (chairman of the Joint Chiefs of Staff, Lyman Lemnitzer) and although it went all the way to President Kennedy's desk for final approval, some insist that it was just a one-time aberration that had no chance of ever going operational. Those who make this claim are not serious students of Network-directed policy. Nonetheless, it's worth looking at the primary argument they offer in defense of their position, which is that Lemnitzer allegedly lost his job for signing off on the plan. (I suspect that you or I would face something a little more severe than unemployment if we conspired to facilitate terror attacks against US targets, but I digress.)

It is true that Lemnitzer, after signing off on Northwoods, was denied another term as chairman of the Joint Chiefs of Staff, but he wasn't jobless for very long. Rather, he was soon appointed Supreme Allied Commander of NATO, and NATO is the organization that, along with the CIA, created and ran Operation Gladio. In other words, Lemnitzer's new post provided him the perfect lawless environment to operate in—where orchestrating violent government coups, engaging in false-flag terrorism, and carrying out assassinations all served to further official Network policy. He wasn't *punished*; he was promoted.

Operation Gladio

> "You had to attack civilians, the people, women, children, innocent people, unknown people far removed from any political game. The reason was quite simple...to force these people...to turn to the State to ask for greater security. This is the political logic that lies behind all the massacres and the bombings which remain unpunished, because the State cannot convict itself or declare itself responsible for what happened."—Vincenzo Vinciguerra, Gladio-linked terrorist[3]

If Operation Gladio had been conceived and directed by the Nazis, most people would have no problem believing every despicable detail. Why? Because most people accept that the Nazis were psychotic criminals who engaged in countless violations of human rights and that they had no respect for freedom or "democracy." Learning of additional crimes wouldn't disrupt the average person's world view at all...far from it. Confirmation bias[4] would kick in, and the individual would experience the psychological rewards of having their world view confirmed.

But what happens when, instead of the Nazis, it's the United States Government that is accused of countless violations of human rights? What happens when the presumed *guardian* of freedom and democracy is accused of

---

3 Daniele Ganser, *NATO's Secret Armies*, page 7
4 "Confirmation bias" refers to people's propensity to accept information that supports what they already believe, especially if their belief is deeply entrenched and emotionally charged.

using terrorism and murder to circumvent both? Now, confirmation bias begins working in reverse. The individual's deeply held beliefs about America's morality are challenged. There are no psychological rewards for even considering the charges, let alone accepting them. Faced with this threat to their world view, many will immediately reject the accusations as ridiculous. They will angrily defend the good name of America and shower the accuser in hatred and condemnation.

The Network knows this. Countless university studies (along with secret operations like MK Ultra) have provided their experts an understanding of human psychology that exceeds anything we can comfortably imagine. They are masters at manipulating the well-meaning public away from scrutinizing their crimes. But there is a key to understanding this particular manipulation; its success relies almost entirely on how the accusation is *framed*. (In this case the more sweeping the accusation, the better it is for the Network.)

In other words, it actually *is* ridiculous to accuse the United States government of facilitating terror attacks when 99.9 percent of the government's employees had no idea what was going on and had no say in the matter. It *is* ridiculous to accuse "America" of supporting ruthless dictators and working to *destroy* freedom around the world when none of the American public was ever asked its opinion on the *policy*.

Though stated in earlier chapters, this point deserves further clarification before we continue: the average government employee, the average American citizen, and the nation as a whole has nothing to do with operations like Gladio. These operations are created and run by the Network, and the Network is composed of criminals in the truest sense of the word. These criminals do not respect "America" or the American form of government. Quite the contrary, they despise it. If permitted to do so, they *will* destroy the US Constitution and Bill of Rights, because the ideals enshrined in these documents are nothing more than a limitation on their power. They *do not* represent the United States or its people.[5]

Unfortunately, it makes no difference whether or not *the people* agree with the Network's policies at this point. Under the current system, public opinion is skillfully manipulated or outright ignored. This is the heart of our problem, and it leads us to a troubling question from Daniele Ganser's book on Operation Gladio:

> If democracy is a system of rules and procedures which define the parameters within which political action can take place, what happens when alongside this system there is another [system] whose rules are mysterious, its procedures unknown, its power immense and which is able to protect itself against the formal institutions of democracy by a wall of secrecy?[6]

That's a pretty easy question to answer. The *hidden* system is where the real power resides. The visible system is only there to maintain the illusion of legitimate government and conceal the hand of those who've taken hold. So let's reveal that hand now.

The CIA created Gladio, in cooperation with British intelligence (MI6), under the pretext of containing the Communist threat. (Even this seemingly valid pretext was a deception, because the Network had been instrumental

---

5 I am not suggesting that we are all blameless, as it is *our job* to police and control the actions of our government. What I am saying is that we must make sure that blame for the Network's crimes is placed precisely where it belongs. Otherwise, the Network can stir an emotional response among the public (by appealing to patriotism) that serves its own interests.

6 *NATO's Secret Armies*, pages 74, 75

in *creating* and sustaining the Communist threat all along,[7] with even deadlier consequences than the Hitler-empowerment project.) Gladio's network of secret armies engaged in "unorthodox warfare" under NATO command. They operated not only in all sixteen NATO countries during the Cold War, but also within the neutral countries of Sweden, Finland, Austria, and Switzerland.[8] The existence of these armies was kept hidden from all but a handful of government personnel within each country. Ganser writes:

> The secret armies were equipped by the CIA and the MI6 with machine guns, explosives, munitions and high-tech communication equipment...Leading officers of the secret network trained together with US Green Berets...and the British SAS Special Forces...The secret armies, as the secondary sources now available suggest, were involved in a whole series of terrorist operations and human rights violations that they wrongly blamed on the Communists in order to discredit the left at the polls. The operations always aimed at spreading maximum fear among the population and ranged from bomb massacres in trains and market squares (Italy), the use of systematic torture of opponents of the regime (Turkey), the support for right-wing coup d'états

---

7 From the IPR's role in Communist China to the Bolshevik Revolution and the rise of the Soviet Union, the "capitalist" Network provided indispensable assistance including financial aid and military technology to their so-called "enemies" in the East. Professor Antony Sutton authored many books documenting the Network's role in the rise of Communism (http://en.wikipedia.org/wiki/Antony_C._Sutton). After decades of research, he eventually declared the Communists "the best enemy money can buy" and he was right. Without the threat of Communism, there would have been no justification for the unprecedented expansion of US military spending and the equally unprecedented acceptance of foreign interventionism. (Today, terrorism has replaced Communism as the Network's go-to pretext.)
8 *NATO's Secret Armies*, page XV

(Greece and Turkey), to the smashing of opposition groups (Portugal and Spain.)[9]

Though these secret armies were allegedly created to protect the Western European democracies from Soviet invasion, they were instead used to interfere with the democratic process whenever the electorate threatened to vote contrary to the Network's desires. This dual policy (claiming to protect national sovereignty and democracy, while simultaneously working to undermine it) was apparently outlined in a secret NATO document dating back to 1949. The document stated that before a nation could join NATO, it had to agree to remain aligned with the "West" *regardless* of what the electorate of the nation wanted.[10] Another top-secret NATO document went further. If the citizens within a nation became so fed up with their puppet NATO leadership that they rose up against it, the US military would come in and suppress the uprising, even if that meant acting *without* the consent of the national government itself.[11]

There are many very disturbing things about Operation Gladio, but perhaps the most disturbing is that the CIA and NATO managed to keep it secret for so long. Despite a long list of murders and atrocities committed by the armies, and by ruthless regimes that the armies supported, both the operation and its architects remained hidden for more than forty years. It wasn't until 1990 that the first on-the-record government disclosure was made, and not because of a desire to come clean, but because former denials could no longer stand.[12] If not for the efforts of an inquisitive Italian

---

9 *NATO's Secret Armies*, pages 1, 2
10 *NATO's Secret Armies*, pages 29, 99
11 *NATO's Secret Armies*, page 185
12 *NATO's Secret Armies*, page 9

judge named Felice Casson, Gladio might never have been exposed.

Uncovering Gladio

In 1984 Judge Felice Casson began digging into an unsolved crime: a car-bomb attack that took place near Peteano, Italy, in 1972. Though the attack killed three police officers and seriously wounded another, the Italian government never managed to find and prosecute the terrorists involved. While conducting his research, Casson discovered a series of suspicious "blunders and fabrications" that had derailed the original investigation. One of those fabrications included a deliberately falsified report about the type of explosive used in the attack. This specific piece of evidence not only led Casson to the man who had planted the bomb, it also led him to the reason *why* the terrorist had escaped punishment for more than a decade.

> Judge Casson...discovered that the report which at the time claimed that the explosive used in Peteano had been the one traditionally used by the [Communist] Red Brigades was a forgery. Marco Morin, an expert for explosives of the Italian police, had deliberately provided fake expertise. He was a member of the Italian right-wing organization "Ordine Nuovo" [New Order] and within the Cold War context contributed his part to what he thought was a legitimate way of combating the influence of the Italian Communists. Judge Casson was able to prove that the explosive used in Peteano contrary to Morin's expertise was C4, the most powerful explosive available at the time, used also by NATO.[13]

---

13 *NATO's Secret Armies*, page 3

Casson's investigation revealed that...Ordine Nuovo had collaborated very closely with the Italian Military Secret Service...Together **they had engineered the Peteano terror** and then wrongly blamed [the Communist] Red Brigades. Judge Casson identified Ordine Nuovo member Vincenzo Vinciguerra as the man who had planted the Peteano bomb... He confessed and testified that he had been covered by an entire network of sympathizers in Italy and abroad who had ensured that after the attack he could escape. "A whole mechanism came into action," Vinciguerra recalled, "[the Italian military police] the Minister of the Interior, the customs services and the military and civilian intelligence services accepted the ideological reasoning behind the attack."[14]

Out of Casson's investigation, and the successful prosecution of Vinciguerra that followed, the Gladio secret finally began to unravel. Unpunished attacks that had terrorized Italian citizens through the 1970s and 1980s were now examined in a new light. The Piazza Fontana massacre of 1969, the 1974 "Italicus Express" attack, the 1980 Bologna railway bomb that killed eighty-five and maimed two hundred: all of these served to further the aims outlined by Vincent Vinciguerra during his sworn testimony in 1984. Keep in mind, Vinciguerra provided his testimony six years *before* the Italian government admitted that the secret armies existed. He described Gladio, including its link to the Italian secret service and NATO, in unequivocal terms:

With the massacre of Peteano, and with all those that have followed, the knowledge should by now be

---

14 *NATO's Secret Armies*, page 4

clear that there existed a real live structure, occult and hidden, with the capacity of giving a strategic direction to the outrages...[it] lies within the state itself...There exists in Italy a secret force parallel to the armed forces, composed of civilians and military men, in an anti-Soviet capacity...A secret organization, a super-organization with a network of communications, arms and explosives, and men trained to use them...A super-organization which...took up the task, on Nato's behalf, of preventing a slip to the left in the political balance of the country.[15]

In another statement Vinciguerra stated:

The terrorist line was followed by camouflaged people, people belonging to the security apparatus, or those linked to the state apparatus through rapport or collaboration. I say that every single outrage that followed from 1969 fitted into a single, organized matrix...Avanguardia Nazionale, like Ordine Nuovo...were being mobilized into the battle as part of an anti-communist strategy **originating not with organizations deviant from the institutions of power, but from within the state itself, and specifically from within the ambit of the state's relations within the [NATO] Atlantic Alliance.**[16]

Although Vinciguerra wasn't the first person to expose Gladio under oath (the former head of the Italian secret service had resentfully confessed ten years earlier[17]), his

---

15 http://en.wikipedia.org/wiki/Vincenzo_Vinciguerra
16 http://en.wikipedia.org/wiki/Vincenzo_Vinciguerra
17 In 1974, another Italian Judge (Giovanni Tamburino) arrested the chief of the Italian secret service (Vito Miceli) on the charge of "promoting, setting up, and organizing...a secret association of military and civilians aimed at [bringing] about an illegal change in the constitution of the state and the form of government." While on

testimony and Casson's further research is what finally broke the story. It forced the Italian prime minister to retract his earlier denials and publicly admit the existence of Gladio to the amazement of citizens and parliamentarians alike.

This watershed moment not only exposed the Network's secret armies in Italy, but it led to the discovery of secret armies in nineteen other countries as well. From the torture and terror in Francisco Franco's Spain (where a former defense minister admitted "here Gladio was the government"[18]), to the assassinations and false flags carried out in Turkey; from the indiscriminant mass shootings of men, women, and children in Belgium,[19] to the imposition of a military dictatorship in Greece, the Network ruthlessly violated the sovereignty of nations while claiming to defend freedom, human rights, and democracy. For insight into the level of hypocrisy, consider this snapshot of what occurred in Greece immediately following the "Gladio coup."

> In the space of some five hours, over 10,000 people were arrested by military squads according to detailed files and planning, and were taken to "reception centers"...Most of those who were arrested in the first hours after the coup were later moved to police and army cells. Communists, Socialists, artists, academics, journalists, students, politically active women, priests, including their friends and families, were tortured. Their toe and fingernails were torn out. Their feet were beaten with sticks until the skin

---

trial, Miceli confessed to setting up the secret army, but furiously replied that it was done under the direction of the United States and NATO. Due to his powerful contacts, Miceli was released on bail and eventually served six months in an Italian military hospital. Reference: *NATO's Secret Armies*, page 8

18 *NATO's Secret Armies*, page 19

19 Known as the "Brabant Massacres," Ganser covers them in *NATO's Secret Armies* on pages 138 through 147

came off and bones were broken...Filthy rags, often soaked in urine, and sometimes excrement, were pushed down their throats..."We are all democrats here"...the chief of the secret police in Athens was fond of stressing. "Everybody who comes here talks. You're not spoiling our record." The sadist torturer made it clear to his victims: "We are the government, you are nothing...The whole world is in two parts, the Russians and the Americans. We are the Americans. Be grateful we've only tortured you a little. In Russia, they'd kill you."[20]

Side Note: It would be bad enough if the Network limited its policy of employing terrorists and propping up ruthless dictators to just Western Europe. But that, of course, would be ridiculous. The Shah in Iran, Augusto Pinochet in Chile, the military junta in Argentina—each of these regimes brutalized their citizens with torture and murder; each of these regimes was brought to power by the Network. Worse still, they represent only a few of the *proven* "regime change actions"[21] conducted by the Network and its instruments in recent history.

These acts of aggression against national sovereignty send a crystal-clear message to any leadership that dares to disobey: resist, and the consequences for you *and the people of your country* could be very dire. Here again the Gladio coup in Greece provides some insight. In 1964 (prior to

---

20 *NATO's Secret Armies*, pages 221 and 222
21 Syria 1949, Iran 1953, Guatemala 1954, Tibet 1955–70s, Indonesia 1958, Cuba 1959, Democratic Republic of the Congo 1960–65, Iraq 1960–63, Dominican Republic 1961, South Vietnam 1963, Brazil 1964, Ghana 1966, Chile 1970–73, Argentina 1976, Afghanistan 1979–89, Turkey 1980, Poland 1980–81, Nicaragua 1981–90, Cambodia 1980–95, Angola 1980s, Philippines 1986, Iraq 1992–96, Afghanistan 2001, Venezuela 2002, Iraq 2002–03, Haiti 2004, Gaza Strip 2006–present, Somalia 2006–07, Iran 2005–present, Libya 2011, Syria 2012–present (See "Covert US Regime Change Actions" at JoePlummer.com/bonus-material)

the coup), the Greek ambassador had rejected Network demands to divide the island nation of Cyprus. Infuriated, President Lyndon Johnson warned: **"Then listen to me, Mr. Ambassador, fuck your parliament and your constitution. America is an elephant. Cyprus is a flea. Greece is a flea...If your Prime Minister gives me talk about democracy, parliament and constitution, he, his parliament and his constitution may not last very long."**[22] In 1967, after some additional "disagreements" with the Network, Greek Gladio carried out Johnson's threat.[23]

Although Operation Gladio was exposed more than twenty years ago, *most* public officials still aren't ready to admit that the Gladio armies facilitated coups, carried out terrorist attacks, or sought to provide "a strategic direction to the outrages." To be fair, there isn't much of an incentive for them to do so. Since we still live in a Network-dominated world, such unflattering statements could bring a wide range of consequences—everything from a ruined career, to torture, to a bullet in the head.[24] However, that's not to say that all public officials have turned their backs on the evidence and remained silent. One of the more-damning indictments came from an Italian investigation in 2000:

> A 2000 Senate report, stated that "Those massacres, those bombs, those military actions had been organized or promoted or supported by men inside Italian state institutions and, as has been discovered more

---

22 *NATO's Secret Armies*, page 219
23 *NATO's Secret Armies*, pages 220, 221
24 In *NATO's Secret Armies*, Ganser covers a number of individuals who were assassinated because they threatened the Gladio program. Here are a couple examples: Renzo Rocca, who participated in the Gladio "silent coup" in Italy, agreed to cooperate with investigators but was assassinated the day before his testimony (reference: pages 71 and 72 of *NATO's Secret Armies*). Major Cem Ersever wrote a book under a fake name that openly discussed false flags and other crimes that he committed in conjunction with "Counter-Guerrilla" (the Turkish Gladio army). Shortly after its publication, he was tortured and shot in the back of the head (reference pages 240 and 241 of *NATO's Secret Armies* and http://en.wikipedia.org/wiki/Cem_Ersever).

recently, by men linked to the structures of United States intelligence." According to *The Guardian,* "The report [claimed] that US intelligence agents were informed in advance about several rightwing terrorist bombings...but did nothing to alert the Italian authorities or to prevent the attacks from taking place."[25]

In 1990, the European Union (EU) parliament "sharply condemned NATO and the United States in a resolution for having manipulated European politics with the stay-behind armies."[26] The parliament called for a full investigation, but the political will to get this done (or maybe the political *power* to get this done) has yet to materialize. Sadly, the EU parliament isn't alone in its lack of resolve. Out of the twenty countries affected by Gladio, only three (Italy, Switzerland, and Belgium) have bothered to conduct a parliamentary investigation.

During the Swiss investigation, Colonel Herbert Alboth (former commander of P-26, the Swiss secret army) sent a confidential letter to a member of the defense department declaring that he was willing to reveal the "whole truth." Soon thereafter, Alboth was found stabbed to death with his own military bayonet.[27] The investigation continued but only yielded a heavily redacted report that said, in part, that the secret army was without "political or legal legitimacy," and that it worked closely with the British secret service who provided "training in combat, communications, and sabotage."[28] This fell far short of what might have come to light if not for Alboth's death and its predictable chilling effect on witnesses and parliamentarians.

---

25 http://en.wikipedia.org/wiki/Operation_Gladio
26 *NATO's Secret Armies,* page 256
27 *NATO's Secret Armies,* page 256 and http://en.wikipedia.org/wiki/Projekt-26#Assassination_of_Herbert_Alboth
28 http://en.wikipedia.org/wiki/Projekt-26#The_Cornu_Report

The Belgian inquiry yielded even less information. Hamstrung from the start by the unwillingness of witnesses to disclose what they knew and made worse by the government's insistence that the commission operate behind closed doors (unlike normal parliamentary inquiries), public and press access to information proved insignificant. In the end, the inquiry "resulted in the preparation of new legislation governing the mission and methods of the Belgian State Security Service and Belgian General Information and Security Service."[29] For lack of a better word, it amounted to a whitewash.

Maybe Switzerland and Belgium are "fleas." Maybe the EU and all of the other nations affected by Gladio are fleas. Maybe these European leaders are so afraid of the Network's "elephant" that they cannot effectively do their job. Ah, but we can't just blame the European leaders for *their* lack of courage. How many US leaders have called for an investigation into Gladio? (Have you ever even heard the word "Gladio" leave the lips of *any* US representative?)

It's likely that less than 1 percent of the US population has heard of Operation Gladio. Even fewer could explain its undeniably antidemocratic and illegal influence on sovereignty. But since the Network is strongest in the United States, a total lack of mainstream coverage and knowledge is predictable. The media, the public schools, the government: all of these instruments constantly profess the sanctity of justice, freedom, and democracy. If US citizens were to get a good look at what their rulers will do to maintain control overseas, they might just start looking into what they will do to maintain control at home. They might just ask themselves: If these criminals will lie, cheat, steal, torture, maim, and murder to control "fleas," what will they do

---

29 http://en.wikipedia.org/wiki/Belgian_stay-behind_network

to maintain control of their elephant, their most cherished and powerful instrument?

Final Note: As early as 1991, the US National Security Archive at George Washington University filed a Freedom of Information Act (FOIA) request regarding the CIA's role in Operation Gladio. In 1995, the Italian senate filed a FOIA request regarding Operation Gladio and the assassination of Prime Minister Aldo Moro. In 1996, Oliver Rathkolb of Vienna University filed a FOIA request regarding Gladio's role in Austria. In 2001 (and beyond), Daniele Ganser has filed FOIA requests regarding the CIA's role in Gladio. In each instance, the CIA has rejected the requests with the standard reply of "The CIA can neither confirm nor deny the existence or nonexistence of records responsive to your request."

In 2006, the State Department tried to dismiss[30] the mountain of evidence presented by Ganser in *NATO's Secret Armies* by challenging the authenticity of *one* very damning document he presents in the book. That document, FM 30-31B, is similar to Operation Northwoods in its shocking content but worse because the false-flag operations described were actually carried out by members of the secret armies. The document was first discovered by a journalist in Turkey seventeen years *prior to* the public admission of Gladio. (That journalist was disappeared before he could provide additional details.) In 1976, after the fall of the Franco/Gladio dictatorship in Spain, excerpts of the document were published in the Spanish press, and in 1978

---

30 http://en.wikipedia.org/wiki/Westmoreland_Field_Manual(Press release). United States Department of State. 2006-01-20. Retrieved 2007-06-24. "A thirty year-old Soviet forgery has been cited as one of the central pieces of 'evidence' for the false notion that West European 'stay-behind' networks engaged in terrorism, allegedly at US instigation. This is not true, and those researching the 'stay behind' networks need to be more discriminating in evaluating the trustworthiness of their source material."

excerpts were also published in Italy.[31] The US government responded promptly, with the help of a "KGB defector," to declare the document a forgery. However, "the discovery in the early 1990s of Operation Gladio in Europe led to renewed debate as to whether or not the manual was fraudulent."[32] In 1992 the former deputy director of the CIA, Ray Cline, confirmed, "This is an authentic document," and Licio Gelli (believed to be a major player in Italian Gladio), stated bluntly, "The CIA gave it to me."[33]

---

31 *NATO's Secret Armies*, page 297, endnote 43
32 http://en.wikipedia.org/wiki/Westmoreland_Field_Manual#Authenticity
33 http://en.wikipedia.org/wiki/Westmoreland_Field_Manual and *NATO's Secret Armies*, pages 234 and 235

CHAPTER 9
Realpolitik Revisited

Though the philosophy of Realpolitik was briefly covered in chapter 1, and though everything written to this point demonstrates the Network's devotion to its principles, nothing captures the cold and calculating nature of its adherents like the false-flag operation. Any willingness to engage in these ruthless deceptions provides definitive proof of an abnormal/sociopathic disregard for ethical considerations.

Normal human beings accept the nearly universal maxim that *morality* determines whether an action is right or wrong. Practitioners of Realpolitik, on the other hand, unapologetically reject this maxim. In their view, right and wrong are measured only in results. If they succeed in securing their objective, what they have done is right. If they fail in securing their objective, what they have done is wrong. They see themselves as *realists,* and dismiss those who criticize the immorality of their actions as impractical fools.

If forced to do so, the realist might offer a moral justification for their immoral actions,[1] but the offer is insincere. Might and manipulation have led them to the apex of power and, as such, they have no incentive to question their

---

1 As noted in chapter 1, Kissinger and other practitioners of Realpolitik claim that their actions cannot be judged as immoral because they are performed in service of the highest good: preservation of the State. But since "the State" is nothing more than those among them who direct the resources and policy of government, their actions are performed in service of their own power and ambition.

approach. They are supremely arrogant. They think and behave differently than you and I; we must be aware of this.

In this final chapter, I hope to remove any doubt about the nature of those we're up against.

Carr, Kissinger, FDR, and Churchill

Perhaps you've heard the joke "If you look up the definition of evil, you'll see a picture of (enter name here) prominently displayed at the top of the page." Well, it's no joke to say, "If you look up the definition of *Realpolitik* at Wikipedia, you'll see Henry Kissinger and E. H. Carr listed as two prominent practitioners."[2] Since Carr is unknown to most, let's begin with him.

E. H. Carr was a highly influential British historian and member of the Network[3] who believed it was *his* role to "work out the basis of a new international order." As a realist, Carr considered the Soviet Union's collectivist/totalitarian system of control far superior to the individualism practiced in the West. In fact, he praised Karl Marx "for emphasizing the importance of the collective over the individual."[4]

> Carr described realism as the acceptance that what exists is right...He argued that in realism there is no moral dimension, and that what is successful is right, and what is unsuccessful is wrong. [As an example, he supported the Bolshevik Revolution based on the grounds of Realpolitik.][5]
>
> In his 1942 book *Conditions of Peace*, Carr argued that it was a flawed economic system that had caused

---

2 http://en.wikipedia.org/wiki/Realpolitik
3 *The Anglo-American Establishment*, page 258
4 http://en.wikipedia.org/wiki/E._H._Carr
5 http://en.wikipedia.org/wiki/Realpolitik

World War II and that the only way of preventing another world war was for the Western powers to fundamentally change the economic basis of their societies by adopting socialism.

In 1945 during a lecture series entitled *The Soviet Impact on the Western World...* Carr argued that "The trend away from individualism and towards totalitarianism is everywhere unmistakable," that Marxism was by far the most successful type of totalitarianism...and that only the "blind and incurable ignored these trends"...Carr claimed that Soviet social policies were far more progressive than Western social policies, and argued democracy was more about social equality than political rights.[6]

Regarding the "more progressive" policies and "social equality" under the Soviet system, Quigley provides some insight:

[For Communism to work in Russia, the Bolsheviks believed that the country needed to be] industrialized at breakneck speed, whatever the waste and hardships...This meant that the goods produced by the peasants must be taken from them...without any economic return, and that the ultimate in authoritarian terror must be used.[7]

All peasants who resisted were treated with violence; their property was confiscated, they were beaten or sent into exile...many were killed. This process, known as "the liquidation of the kulaks"... affected five million kulak families.[8]

---

6 http://en.wikipedia.org/wiki/E._H._Carr
7 *Tragedy and Hope,* page 396
8 *Tragedy and Hope,* page 398

The ordinary Russian had inadequate food and housing, was subject to extended rationing...and was reduced to living, with his family, in a single room or even, in many cases, to a corner of a single room shared with other families. The privileged rulers and their favorites had the best of everything, including foods and wines, the use of vacation villas in the country...the use of official cars in the city, the right to live in old czarist palaces and mansions.[9]

As public discontent and social tensions grew... the use of spying, purges, torture, and murder increased out of all proportion...By the middle 1930's the search for "saboteurs" and for "enemies of the state"...left hardly a family untouched. **Hundreds of thousands were killed**, frequently on completely false charges, while **millions** were arrested and exiled to Siberia or put into huge slave-labor camps. In these camps, under conditions of semi-starvation and incredible cruelty, millions toiled... Estimates of the number of persons (prior to 1941) vary from as low as two million to as high as twenty million. **The majority of these prisoners had done nothing**...[they] consisted of relatives, associates, and friends of persons who had been arrested on more serious charges. Many of these charges were completely false, having been trumped up to provide labor in remote areas, scapegoats for administrative breakdowns, and to eliminate possible rivals in the control of the Soviet system.[10]

Carr not only admired the greater *social equality* that citizens enjoyed under the Soviet regime, he argued that "China was much better off under the leadership of Mao

9 *Tragedy and Hope,* page 401
10 *Tragedy and Hope,* page 402

Zedong..."[11] Mao, of course, was the Network's most successful monster of all. He murdered between eighteen million and thirty-two million human beings during his collectivist *Great Leap Forward.* ("Coercion, terror, and systematic violence were the very foundation of the Great Leap Forward" and it "motivated one of the most deadly mass killings of human history."[12])

Needless to say, Carr was also an enthusiastic supporter of the Hitler-empowerment project. Germany under Hitler, Russia under the Bolsheviks and Stalin, China under Mao—they all share the one characteristic that underpins the realist's political philosophy: might makes right.

Side Note: Any political system that subordinates the rights of the individual to some "greater good" like the *collective* is irresistible to a realist. That's because it not only empowers the realist, but it conceals their power grab (and blatant hypocrisy) in the process. Consider the absurdity of the following scheme: by loudly condemning the selfishness of the evil *individual,* and by praising the selfless virtue of the so-called *collective,* realists can build a system that (far from being administered by or for the benefit of the collective), transfers nearly absolute power to a handful of the most dishonest, selfish, and evil *individuals* that realism can produce.

While Carr overlooked the Network-sponsored horrors of Marxism, Nazism, and Maoism, he continued to enthusiastically denounce the injustices of individualism in the Western world. So what exactly was he up to? Carr either suffered from an incurable case of intellectual inconsistency, or he was a very bold practitioner of Realpolitik...or maybe it was a little of both. All that's certain is if we agree

---

11 http://en.wikipedia.org/wiki/EH_Carr
12 http://en.wikipedia.org/wiki/Great_leap_forward

to surrender our individual "political rights" as men like Carr would have us do, the Network will gladly construct "the basis of a new international order" for us to enjoy. Its members will fulfill their long-standing promise of "social equality" for all. Then, we can finally live in a world where everyone is *equally* powerless to resist their sociopathic conspiracies.

A Pretext for Every Policy

Speaking of sociopathic conspiracies, Operation Gladio demonstrates just how far the Network's realists were willing to go in order to subvert the democratic process in Europe. By using the threat of Communism (which they nurtured), and terrorist attacks (which they facilitated), these skilled practitioners of Realpolitik successfully manipulated everyone involved: the Gladio operatives, the citizens, the government, and the media. To summarize:

First, the Network recruited a handful of Nazis, terrorists, and other hardcore criminals[13] and told them that, to help fight Communism, they would be armed, paid, and protected as they operated above the law. These Gladio operatives proceeded to commit acts of terrorism against innocent people, which, predictably, drove citizens to "turn to the State" for greater security. Unaware of Gladio, well-meaning government officials and reporters accepted and repeated the lie that Communists were behind the murders. This lie, backed by public fear and outrage, was used to increase the power of the state and crack down on individuals identified as Communists or Communist sympathizers. (Any politician, citizen, or group of individuals who challenged the Network's agenda could easily be smeared with these labels.)

---

13 See *NATO's Secret Armies* for the Rouges Gallery of characters recruited and employed by the CIA and NATO during Gladio.

Each step of the way, the "Communist threat" provided a single pretext for the Network's brazen global attack on national sovereignty. If this threat didn't exist, they would have needed to create it.

Unfortunately, this tactic of *creating* pretexts in the form of an enemy, a crisis, or an attack (or all of the above) remains incredibly effective. The average person is unlikely to suspect, let alone accuse, "their own government" of doing something so vile. Not only because it exceeds the socially acceptable limits of distrust, but because the truth, at first, is psychologically intolerable. But these mental barriers must be overcome. If they aren't, *realists* within the Network will continue to employ false flags and similar deceptions. They will continue to do so for the simple reason that these tactics work.

In closing, we'll expand on this idea of *creating* pretexts, starting with Henry Kissinger's take on the matter.

Pawns in the Great Game

The US "elephant" serves no useful purpose to the Network if the traditionally "isolationist" American people can maintain control of that elephant. Sadly, Americans have yet to realize that what *they want* is secondary in importance to what the Network decides they shall have, and this is especially true when it comes to war. Working backward from Vietnam to WWII and then to WWI, this becomes abundantly clear. (In each case the American people were lied to. They were told what they *wanted to hear*, as policy makers secretly conspired against them.)

Beginning with Vietnam, Kissinger concedes that the pretext for sending fifty-five thousand Americans to their death (the Gulf of Tonkin "attack") wasn't based on "a full presentation of the facts." However, he minimizes the relevance of the deception by saying it really wasn't "a major factor in America's commitment to ground combat in Vietnam." While President Johnson assured the public that he wasn't seeking a wider war,[14] the exact opposite was true. Policy makers had already decided against the wishes of the electorate, and that decision would have led us to all-out war, one way or another.[15]

Ray McGovern, a former CIA analyst and later a harsh critic of the agency, described the escalation to war in Vietnam this way:

> During the summer of 1964, President Johnson and the Joint Chiefs of Staff were eager to widen the war in Vietnam. They stepped up sabotage and hit-and-run attacks on the coast of North Vietnam.
>
> Those of us in intelligence, not to mention President Lyndon Johnson, Defense Secretary Robert McNamara, and National Security Adviser McGeorge Bundy, all knew full well that the evidence of any armed attack on the evening of Aug. 4, 1964, the so-called "second" Tonkin Gulf incident, was highly dubious. But it fit the president's purposes, so they lent a hand to facilitate escalation of the war.
>
> In Bamford's words, the Joint Chiefs of Staff had become "a sewer of deceit," with Operation Northwoods and other unconscionable escapades to their credit. Then-Undersecretary of State George Ball commented, "There was a feeling that if the destroyer got into some trouble, that this would provide the provocation we needed."[16]

14 http://en.wikipedia.org/wiki/Gulf_of_Tonkin_Resolution
15 *Diplomacy*, pages 658 and 659
16 http://www.antiwar.com/mcgovern/?articleid=12207

Here we have two concepts that should be familiar by now: one, the tactic of blaming a nonexistent attack on an enemy and using it as a pretext, and, two, provoking a *real attack* and using *that* as a pretext. Although Kissinger disingenuously pins these tactics of manipulation on the puppets who sign off on them, at least he admits they are real. Defending Johnson's deceptive pretext for invading Vietnam, Kissinger informs his readers that FDR did the same thing during WWII:

> Neither Johnson's tactics nor his candor was significantly different from Franklin Delano Roosevelt's when he had edged America toward involvement in the Second World War—for example, Roosevelt's not altogether candid account of the torpedoing of the destroyer *Greer*, the pretext for engaging America in a naval war in the Atlantic…**Both presidents were prepared to put their country's military forces in harm's way and to respond should harm indeed befall them, as was likely. In each case, the ultimate decision to enter the war was based on considerations which went far beyond the immediate incidents.**[17]

Regarding the *Greer*,[18] Roosevelt had made a clash "inevitable" when he ordered US ships to report the position of German submarines to the British Navy."[19] The Greer, on the day it was attacked, had spent hours chasing after and reporting the location of an Axis submarine as the British dropped depth charges from the air. This pursuit continued for nearly three hours and thirty minutes before the sub fired its first torpedo. The *Greer* then continued its

---

17 *Diplomacy*, page 659
18 http://en.wikipedia.org/wiki/USS_Greer_(DD-145)
19 *Diplomacy*, 392

pursuit for another five hours, dropping depth charges of its own, before continuing on its scheduled course.

Roosevelt promptly reported the torpedo attack to the public, but he made no mention of the circumstances that preceded it.[20] Instead, he dishonestly presented the incident as an unprovoked "act of piracy" and used it as a pretext for a radical new "shoot-on-sight" policy. This, in Kissinger's own words, "crossed the line into belligerency." Under this policy, any Axis submarine, whether it attacked a US ship or not, was to be fired on as if it *had* attacked.[21] Though undeclared and limited, this essentially put America at war against the Axis powers.

But *limited* warfare was never the goal. The Network intended to drag the United States fully into WWII regardless of the American public's desire to remain neutral. And while the attack on the *Greer* moved US policy and opinion in the "right" direction, the devastating attack on Pearl Harbor sealed the deal.

On this topic, Kissinger is a little more cautious about describing FDR's willingness to put US ships and military personnel "in harm's way." For instance, he doesn't mention the McCollum memo, which recommended "an eight-part course of action for the United States to take" in order to provoke Japan into "committing an overt act of war."[22] However, he does mention a few of the "pressures" (outlined in the McCollum memo) that were placed on Japan prior to the Pearl Harbor attack. Additionally, he hints at the provocation when he says "few understood *the nature of the diplomacy* that had preceded Japan's attack on Pearl Harbor...It was a measure of the United States' deep seated

20 The audio of FDR's fireside chat about the *Greer* is available here: http://youtu.be/fUWJX-j1xws
21 http://en.wikipedia.org/wiki/USS_Greer_(DD-145)
22 http://en.wikipedia.org/wiki/McCollum_memo

isolationism that it **had to be bombed at Pearl Harbor** before it would enter the war in the Pacific."[23]

FDR's repeated assurances to the American people that the nation would be kept out of the war were nothing more than dual policy. Kissinger praises FDR's cunning when he writes:

> America's entry into the war marked the culmination of a great and daring leader's extraordinary diplomatic enterprise. In less than three years, Roosevelt had taken his staunchly isolationist people into a global war...Roosevelt had achieved his goal patiently and inexorably, educating his people one step at a time about the necessities before them... By initiating hostilities, the Axis powers had solved Roosevelt's lingering dilemma about how to move the American people into the war.[24]

Just to be clear, there is some misdirection in Kissinger's statement. It wasn't really *FDR* who maneuvered the "staunchly isolationist" American people into WWII. That credit more appropriately belongs to the Network. FDR, like every president after Woodrow Wilson, served a power much greater than himself. He was little more than the public face of the Network's global policy.

Having covered the pretexts for Vietnam and WWII, this brings us to the "surprise attack" on the passenger liner *Lusitania* that served as the pretext for US entry into WWI.

Sink the *Lusitania*

Recall from chapter 6 that, just prior to WWI, the Network concluded that war is the most effective way to "alter the life

23 *Diplomacy*, page 393
24 *Diplomacy*, pages 392, 393

of an entire people." Though the stage for WWI was already set, the staunchly isolationist tendencies of the United States posed a problem. To overcome this problem, the Network set out to gain "control of the State Department" and the "diplomatic machinery" of America. It achieved this by bringing Woodrow Wilson to power in 1913. More accurately, the Network achieved this by bringing Wilson's *advisor*, Mandell House, to power. As House's biographer notes: "It was House who made the slate for the Cabinet, formulated the first policies of the Administration and *practically* directed the foreign affairs of the United States."[25] (If you do a little research into Mandell House, you'll soon realize that the word "practically" does not belong in the preceding sentence.)

After all of the right people and instruments were in place (including the Network's two newly created funding mechanisms[26]), a secret society known as the Black Hand entered the picture. In June 1914 it ordered the assassination of Archduke Franz Ferdinand and, within a month, WWI was underway.[27] From that point forward, the final steps were clear: maximize the duration and costs of the war, drag the United States into the conflict by whatever means necessary, and then allow the carefully chosen puppet (Wilson) to sell "his" vision for a New World Order.

The first problem the Network faced was making sure that the war didn't end too quickly. As early as February 1915, Wilson's talk of "peace" was threatening to end hostilities. Worse, to encourage a dialogue between the

---

25 As quoted in *The Creature from Jekyll Island*, page 240
26 The Federal Reserve System and the federal income tax
27 "Black Hand trained guerillas and saboteurs and planned political murders." The Black Hand's "Executive Committee was led, more or less, by Colonel Dragutin Dimitrijević." Reference: https://en.wikipedia.org/wiki/Black_Hand_(Serbia) "When Dimitrijević heard that Archduke Franz Ferdinand was planning to visit Sarajevo in June 1914, he sent three members of the Young Bosnia group...to assassinate him. At this time, Dimitrijević was Chief of Serbian Military Intelligence." Reference: http://en.wikipedia.org/wiki/Dragutin_Dimitrjevic_Apis

warring nations, President Wilson sent Mandell House to London and instructed House to "bear the President's... profound hope that the war could be ended quickly." However, during his trip, House conveyed the exact *opposite* of the president's sentiments. In his London meeting with Sir Edward Grey, House assured Grey that he had "no intention of pushing the issue of peace"[28] and, in so doing, intentionally undermined any prospect of mediation. Professor Knock informs us that:

> In certain critical instances, "Phillip Dru" seemed to overpower [House]. His statement to Grey hardly reflected Wilson's position. To the contrary, House often expressed unabashedly pro-Allied sentiments...and firmly believed that the basis for future peace lay in an Anglo-American entente. He never accurately informed Wilson about this part of his conversation with Grey; while thus gaining the Foreign Secretary's trust, he obviously did not serve his own chief very well.[29]

House might have proven himself to Edward Grey (an imperialist Network insider), but this particular diplomatic maneuver was not sufficient to ensure the continuation of hostilities, let alone ensure that the United States would enter the war. For that, the public would have to be manipulated. Some of them might even have to be "put in harm's way." And here is where the British passenger liner *Lusitania* enters the picture.

There isn't enough room to tell the full story here, but suffice to say, the case of the *Lusitania* was a "damn dirty

28 *To End All Wars*, pages 45, 46
29 *To End All Wars*, page 46

business."[30] Consider the following a short summary. For a more thorough account, I highly recommend that you read chapter 12 of *The Creature from Jekyll Island.*

Let's begin with the fact that although the *Lusitania* was considered a luxury passenger liner, its design specifications were drawn up by the British Admiralty. This enabled the British to easily convert her into a ship of war. In 1913, after adding armor and some other modifications, the British did exactly that. Unbeknownst to her passengers, the ship was then entered into the Admiralty fleet register as an *armed auxiliary cruiser.* Despite US "neutrality" and the risk to those aboard:

> The *Lusitania* became one of the most important carriers of war materials—including munitions—from the United States to England...On March 8th 1915... the captain of the *Lusitania* turned in his resignation...he was no longer willing "to carry the responsibility of mixing passengers with munitions."[31]

Winston Churchill, unlike the captain of the *Lusitania,* had absolutely no problem mixing passengers with munitions. In fact the careless mixing of passengers, especially *American* passengers, with war materials could prove very useful politically. For instance, in the event that Germans attacked a "passenger liner" with men, women, and children aboard—*American* men, women, and children—the beneficial effect on American public opinion would be swift and unanimous. After a handful of stern government condemnations and a well-orchestrated media campaign, it

---

30 Lord Mersey was charged with determining the facts surrounding the sinking of the *Lusitania.* Under pressure, he issued the report that was expected of him but refused compensation and requested that he no longer be called upon to "administer His Majesty's Justice." His final statement on the affair was: "The *Lusitania* case was a damn dirty business" (as quoted in *The Creature from Jekyll Island*, page 255).
31 *The Creature from Jekyll Island*, pages 247, 248

would be easy to shame the isolationists into silence while moving the United States toward entering the war.

Much like FDR's policy with the *Greer*, Churchill's orders (to load munitions onto passenger ships) made a clash at sea inevitable. But this wasn't the only way to provoke a politically useful attack. To increase the likelihood of innocent civilian casualties, Churchill ordered British merchant ships to ram German subs if they attempted to stop and search them for contraband. This made it impossible for Germany to observe the long-established Cruiser Rules. (Under the Cruiser Rules, an unarmed merchant vessel would *not* be sunk until the crew and passengers were safely evacuated from the ship.) With Churchill's new policy in place, German submarines could no longer come to the surface and were more apt to sink ships without warning. As the following quote from Churchill demonstrates, this was his intention from the start.

> The first British countermove, made on my responsibility…was to deter the Germans from surface attack. The submerged U-boat had to rely increasingly on underwater attack and thus **ran the greater risk of mistaking neutral for British ships and of drowning neutral crews and thus embroiling Germany with other Great Powers.**[32]

And yet, even these measures proved insufficient to bring about the *Lusitania*'s demise. It wasn't until the ship was intentionally sent into hostile waters at reduced speed and with her military escort withdrawn that Churchill, and the Network he served, secured their pretext. Griffin writes:

---

32 As quoted in *The Creature from Jekyll Island*, page 249

In the map room of the British Admiralty, Churchill watched the play unfold and coldly called the shots. Small disks marked the places where two ships had been torpedoed the day before. A circle indicated the area within which the U-boat must still be operating. A larger disk represented the *Lusitania* travelling at nineteen knots directly into the circle... Commander Joseph Kenworthy, who previously had been called upon by Churchill to submit a paper on what would be the political results of an ocean liner being sunk with American passengers aboard...left the room in disgust.

Colonel House was in England at that time and, on the day of the sinking...Sir Edward Grey asked him: "What will America do if the Germans sink an ocean liner with American passengers on board?" As recorded in House's diaries, he replied: "I told him if this were done, a flame of indignation would sweep America, which would in itself probably carry us into the war."...King George also brought up the subject and was even more specific about the possible target. He asked, "Suppose they should sink the *Lusitania* with American passengers on board...?[33]

Approximately four hours later, a torpedo sent the *Lusitania* to the bottom of the ocean. Of its 1,959 passengers, 1,198 lost their lives. Nearly all of the US citizens aboard (128 of 139) were killed.[34] Predictably, House immediately seized the opportunity to stoke the "flame of indignation," while cynically appealing to the moral implications of continued US neutrality.

33 *The Creature from Jekyll Island*, page 253
34 http://en.wikipedia.org/wiki/Rms_lusitania

From England, Colonel House sent a telegram to President Wilson...It became the genesis of thousands of newspaper editorials across the land. He said piously:

"America has come to the parting of the ways, when she must determine whether she stands for civilized or uncivilized warfare. We can no longer remain neutral spectators. Our action in this crisis will determine...how far we may influence a settlement for the lasting good of humanity...our position amongst nations is being assessed by mankind."

In another telegram two days later, House reveals himself as the master psycho-politician playing on Wilson's ego like a violinist stroking the strings of a Stradivarius. He wrote:

"If, unhappily, it is necessary to go to war, I hope you will give the world an exhibition of American efficiency that will be a lesson for a century or more. It is generally believed throughout Europe that we are so unprepared...that our entering would make but little difference...In the event of war, we should accelerate the manufacture of munitions to such an extent that we could supply not only ourselves but the Allies, and so quickly that the world would be astounded."[35]

Regarding propaganda efforts overseas, Quigley adds:

The propaganda agencies...made full use of the occasion. *The Times* of London announced that "four-fifths of her passengers were citizens of the United States"...the British *manufactured* and distributed a medal which they pretended had been awarded to

---

35 *The Creature from Jekyll Island,* page 257

the submarine crew by the German government; a French paper published a picture of the crowds in Berlin at the outbreak of war in 1914 as a picture of Germans "rejoicing" at the news of the sinking of the *Lusitania*.[36]

The end of this story holds no surprises. Less than a year later, in cooperation with House and Sir Edward Grey, President Wilson signed off on a scheme[37] that would drag the United States into World War I. The president did this without the knowledge of the United States Senate and, of course, without the knowledge of the American people. He then proceeded to campaign for his reelection under the slogan "He Kept Us out of the War," patiently waiting until he'd secured his second term before entering World War I in April 1917.

The moment Wilson declared war, vast amounts of money began flowing directly into the Network's coffers. Adjusted for inflation, the total cost to the United States from 1917 to 1919 would equal more than $500 billion today. This "war to end all wars" not only buried the United States in debt, it increased the Network's financial leverage in direct proportion to that debt.[38] But there were additional *profits* as well. Competing empires were destroyed, the

---

36 *Tragedy and Hope,* page 251

37 From *The Creature from Jekyll Island,* page 242: "The basic terms of the agreement were that the United States government would offer to negotiate a peaceful settlement between Germany and the Allies...If either side refused to accept the proposal, then the United States would come into the war as an ally of the other side. The catch was that the terms of the proposal were carefully drafted so that Germany could not possibly accept them. Thus, to the world, it would look as though Germany was at fault and the United States was humanitarian."

38 Recall from chapter 6: "As payments on mounting debt create greater and greater shortfalls, and as annual spending continues to increase unabated, larger and more frequent loans become necessary to bridge the gap. This accelerates the rate at which the national debt grows and, before long, even powerful nations will find themselves utterly dependent on a constant flow of newly borrowed funds to cover their expenses." The Network is always happy to supply those funds with more debt money that they create out of thin air.

isolationist tendencies of the United States were subverted, and the initial framework for a New World Order took shape. None of this happened by chance; each and every step was carefully planned to yield the desired result. And there you see how a handful of false and designing men can manipulate entire nations and alter the history of the world.

A Century of Deception, Theft, and Violence

We've covered an awful lot of ground in the pages of this short book: from the origins of the Network's secret society to its sovereignty-destruction project and "ultimate recovery of the United States of America" in 1913[39]; from the blatant fraud of its primary funding mechanisms[40] to its use of ruthless dictators, dual policies, and false-flag operations. What can be said of these men who've achieved so much at the expense of so many? Have they *earned* the power that they possess? Have we *earned* the consequences of allowing them to dominate us?

The Network believes that the key to controlling the world lies in the application of "***secret*** political and economic influence" and secret control of "journalistic, educational, and propaganda agencies."[41] Based on their impressive list of global accomplishments, it certainly appears as if they're right. But what happens if their secret "influence" and tactics are exposed for all to see? Could they continue to get away with their crimes? Could they continue to manipulate us into wars, bury us beneath inescapable debt, and con us into surrendering our

---

39 Referencing the stated goal of the Network's founder, Cecil Rhodes, as quoted in *The Anglo-American Establishment*, page 33

40 As covered in chapter 4, the two primary funding mechanisms are the Federal Reserve System and federal income tax, both of which were "sold" to the public via deception in 1913.

41 *The Anglo-American Establishment*, page 49

sovereignty? The answer, by their own estimation, is no. When *what* they're doing and *how* they're doing it becomes widely known, the foundation on which their success is built crumbles beneath them.

Fortunately, this means that the most important work we can do is also the *easiest*. To the extent we expose the origin and purpose of their instruments, their tried-and-true tactics of manipulation, and their immoral belief that only *might* determines what's right, we destroy the illusion of legitimacy that they depend on. "So long as we are gaining and spreading awareness, they (by default) are losing power."[42] This is where we must begin. This is the first step toward destroying their system. So please,

> Reach out to new people regularly and share information that exposes what the Network is and how it operates. When you encounter individuals who either refuse to look at the facts, or who minimize the significance of what's presented, do not take it personally. If they attack you, do not take it personally. In most cases, they are simply defending their world view...it has nothing to do with you. Simply move on and know that every single person that is exposed to this information, even those who initially resist, could become an ally down the road. The same cannot be said of those who are never exposed to the truth.[43]

---

42 http://joeplummer.com/we_have_the_advantage.html
43 *Tragedy and Hope 101*, chapter 5, Solution #1

Final Thoughts

In May 2012 I began sorting through and organizing the reference material for this book. After a couple months of narrowing my choices, I came to a reasonably depressing conclusion: there was absolutely no way I could adequately condense Quigley's work into just a couple hundred pages, let alone condense the Network-coordinated depravity exposed in the dozens of other excellent books[1] that I wanted to cover.

By August 2012, it looked like a bomb had gone off in our house; notes and books were strewn everywhere, and counted among the scraps of paper were countless abandoned outlines. With no idea where to begin, and facing thousands of hours of additional work, I nearly put everything away. I'd convinced myself that my best effort would only come up short, so why bother? Ironically, one of the many topics that I knew I couldn't adequately cover, summarized in a couple sentences that I'd scribbled on a piece of paper, started moving me (psychologically) back in the right direction:

How many of us do *nothing* because we feel that we cannot do enough?

How much "more than enough" could be done if all of us simply did *something*?

---

1 See the "recommended-reading" list on the last page

These two sentences led me to reevaluate the reason for writing this book. So what if I couldn't "adequately" summarize all of the material that I wanted to cover? Even an *inadequate* summary would be better than no summary at all. And was this *really* about writing a condensed version of a thirteen-hundred-page history book, or was it more about protecting myself and others from men who believe "there is no moral dimension…what is successful is right"? Clearly it was the latter, and this is what ultimately drove me to continue: a burning desire to expose and weaken the criminal ruling class.

At this point, I can only hope that you share my desire and that you feel the information you've read here is useful. If so, I would ask that you **please tell people about the *free* online version of this book available at TragedyAndHope.INFO**, or if you have a hard copy, share it with friends and family. Take a few minutes and leave a short review at Amazon.com and other websites, or simply recommend the book on message boards if the topic is a good match. Never underestimate the impact you can have each time that you do something.

On my end, I will be creating a "bonus material" section at the TragedyAndHope.INFO website. This will enable me to post my page-reference notes for *Tragedy and Hope*, as well as my notes for *The Anglo-American Establishment, Diplomacy, NATO's Secret Armies,* and some of the other books listed on the following page. These page-reference notes will help you quickly find interesting reference material within each book.

I will also provide links to excellent articles like "The Horrifying American Roots of Nazi Eugenics" available here http://hnn.us/article/1796 . From there I can post related information, like how the *government* (following a 1974 policy report directed by Henry Kissinger) implemented a secret twenty-five-year plan to reduce global fertility,[2] or how the Network, in cooperation with the "government," created genetically modified corn that was designed to sterilize those who ate it and a "tetanus" vaccine designed to sterilize those who received the shot.[3]

These and other topics were too much to squeeze between the covers of this book. Therefore, the bonus-material section will provide interested readers an opportunity to dig deeper into the Network's long list of unpunished crimes. And on that note, if you're ready to start digging now, here are just a handful of books that address the Network's illegitimate power in one way or another. Many of them are available for free online. I've listed them by page count from shortest to longest.

---

2 See National Security Study Memorandum 200, http://en.wikipedia.org/wiki/NSSM_200

3 Paraphrasing William Engdahl's *Seeds of Destruction*, pages 270–275. **Spermicidal corn**: In September 2001 Epicyte reported that they had successfully created the ultimate GMO crop—contraceptive corn. On October 6, 2002, CBS News reported that the United States Department of Agriculture had financed thirty-two field trials including Epicyte's spermicidal corn. What was not revealed was that the USDA was also providing the field trial results to scientists at the US Department of Defense through one of their biological research laboratories. At the time of their brief public announcement, which they presented as a contribution to the world's "overpopulation" problem, Epicyte estimated its spermicidal corn would be available in 2006 or 2007. After the press release, discussion of the breakthrough vanished. Nothing more was heard in any media about the development. **Antifertility vaccines**: The folks at the Rockefeller Foundation, in cooperation with World Health Organization researchers, sought to develop a double-whammy vaccine. In the early 1990s, according to a report from the Global Vaccine Institute, the World Health Organization oversaw massive vaccination campaigns against tetanus in Nicaragua, Mexico, and the Philippines. Numerous vials of the vaccine, tested under suspicion, were found to contain hCG, which, when combined with a tetanus toxoid carrier, renders women incapable of maintaining a pregnancy. Also, rather curiously, this vaccination campaign against "tetanus" was directed only at women of child-bearing ages between fifteen and forty-five. (The men and boys apparently didn't need tetanus protection.) "Pro Vida dug further and learned that the Rockefeller Foundation...the World Bank, the UN Development Program and the Ford Foundation, and others had been working with the World Health Organization for 20 years to develop an anti-fertility vaccine using hCG with tetanus as well as other vaccines." None of the women who received the hCG-laced vaccines were told of the vaccine's abortive properties or its long-term effect on their ability to have children.

Recommended Reading

War Is a Racket, by Major General Smedley Butler

The Law, by Frederic Bastiat

Media Control, by Noam Chomsky

Dumbing Us Down, by John Taylor Gatto

The Impact of Science on Society, by Bertrand Russell

None Dare Call It Conspiracy, by Gary Allen

Philip Dru: Administrator, by Edward Mandell House

Our Enemy the State, by Albert Jay Nock

Propaganda, by Edward Bernays

The Scientific Outlook, by Bertrand Russell

The Shadows of Power, by James Perloff

Confessions of an Economic Hitman, by John Perkins

The Fluoride Deception, by Christopher Bryson

NATO'S Secret Armies, by Daniele Ganser

A Century of War, by William Engdahl

The Case Against Fluoride, by Paul Connett, James Beck, and H. Spedding Micklem

To End all Wars, by Thomas Knock

The Molecular Vision of Life, by Lily E. Kay

The Virus and the Vaccine, by Debbie Bookchin and Jim Schumacher

The Anglo-American Establishment, by Carroll Quigley

Eugenics: A Reassessment, by Richard Lynn

Seeds of Destruction, by William Engdahl

1984, by George Orwell

Blood Bankers, by James Henry

Foundations: Their Power and Influence, by Rene A. Wormser

War Against the Weak, by Edwin Black

Politics in Healing: The Suppression and Manipulation of American Medicine, by Daniel Haley

The Plutonium Files: America's Secret Medical Experiments in the Cold War, by Eileen Welsome

The Pinochet File, by Peter Kornbluh

The Creature from Jekyll Island, by G. Edward Griffin

Diplomacy, by Henry Kissinger

Tragedy and Hope, by Carroll Quigley

Index

Page numbers followed by "n" indicate footnotes.

Strong, Benjamin, 77
Subcommittee on Internal
    Security, 8
submarines and U-boats,
    189–190, 198
Sutton, Anthony, 169n7
Switzerland, 169, 177–178
Syria, 161

Taft, William Howard, 61–66
Tamburino, Giovanni, 173n17
tax-exempt foundations, 13,
    73, 111, 121–122
TenthAmendmentCenter.com,
    114
terrorism, 131–132, 131n14,
    153, 161–162, 163–180,
    169n7, 179n30, 183,
    185–186
terrorists, 161
Tolkein, R. R., 29
Toynbee, Arnold J., 47
Toynbee Hall, 36
Tragedy and Hope (Quigley).
    See also *specific topics of
    discussion*
  overview, 3–6
  publication and suppression
    of, 2–3
transparency, 26, 96, 100
Treaty of Versailles, 141, 151–152

U-boats and submarines,
    195–196

Union of South Africa, 42.
    See also South Africa
United Nations, 157, 159
US Constitution, 27, 51, 54, 73,
    112, 120–121, 160, 168
useful idiot, 58, 58n27
US Senate, 6–7, 137, 176, 198
US State Department, 10,
    122–123, 123n6, 179,
    179m30, 192

value, 95–96
Vanderlip, Frank A., 81, 83–84
Van Zyl, Lizzie, 38–39, 42
Vietnam war, 187–188
Vinciguerra, Vincenzo, 166,
    172–173

Wall Street, 5–6, 8, 75
War and Peace Studies (CFR),
    123, 123n6
Warburg, 48, 80, 84
Ward, Chester, 48
war on freedom, 121–125
Washington Post, 5
Wilson, Woodrow, 45, 53–66,
    73, 78, 83–84, 123, 132–139,
    133n19, 134n20, 191–193,
    197–198
World War I, 66, 87–88, 123,
    132–138, 148, 198
World War II, 132, 138, 141–162,
    183, 189
Wormser, Rene A., 13

Lightning Source UK Ltd.
Milton Keynes UK
UKHW01f1846081018
330211UK00028B/1871/P